SMART ASSETS

SMART ASSETS

Turning You and Your Business into a Wealth Machine

GEORGE D. BRENNER, JD, CLU, ChFC

JOHN T. CECERE, CLU

STANFIELD HILL, JD, CLU

BARRY L. RABINOVICH, JD, AEP

Revised Edition

Co-published with MONY which underwrote the nations first mutual life insurance policy in 1843.

McGraw-Hill
New York San Francisco Washington D.C. Auckland Bogotá
Caracas Lisbon London Madrid Mexico City Milan
Montreal New Delhi Singapore
Sydney Tokyo Toronto

Library of Congress Cataloging-in-Publication Data
Smart assets : turning you and your business into a wealth machine /
    George D. Brenner . . . [et al.].
        p.   cm
      "Co-published with Mutual of New York."
      Includes index.
      ISBN 0-07-007652-9
      1. Small business—finance.   2. Asset-liability management.
    3. Self-employed—Finance, Personal.   I. Brenner, George D.
    HG4027.7.S647   1998
    658.15'92—dc21   98-11449

McGraw-Hill

*A Division of The **McGraw·Hill** Companies*

1 2 3 4 5 6 7 8 9 0 DOC/DOC 9 0 2 1 0 9 8 7

ISBN 0-07-007652-9

The sponsoring editor for this book was Jeffrey Krames and the production supervisor
was Suzanne W. B. Rapcavage. It was set in New Century Schoolbook by Electronic
Publishing Services, Inc.

Printed and bound by R. R. Donnelley & Sons Company.

The previous edition of this book was published under the title *Smart Assets,* by
IRWIN Professional Publishing.

This publication is designed to provide accurate and authoritative information in
regard to the subject matter covered. It is sold with the understanding that neither the
author nor the publisher is engaged in rendering legal, accounting, or other professional service. If legal advice or other expert assistance is required, the services of a
competent professional person should be sought.

> —*From a Declaration of Principles jointly adopted by a Committee of
> the American Bar Association and a Committee of Publishers.*

PREFACE

Asked for his sage advice on the roller-coaster ride of traditional investing, Mark Twain made the following observation:

> October. This is one of the peculiarly dangerous months to speculate in stocks. The others are July, January, September, April, November, May, March, June, December, August, and February.

Clearly, the great American humorist was making his comments with tongue firmly in cheek. Nevertheless, he was touching on an important point: In seeking to make money and accumulate personal wealth, you can work hard or work smart. As most of you have likely discovered, *playing the market*—and making money at it—is harder than it looks, as are most of the widely pursued money-making strategies.

Which brings us to the guiding principle of this book: *Working smart, rather than hard, is the most effective way to build your wealth.* As a small business owner, you have exceptional opportunities to turn yourself and your business into a wealth machine.

How do you accomplish this? By employing one or more of a range of financial strategies—created by tax, estate and business planning, and investment experts—that are designed to capitalize on opportunities to build and protect assets. In many cases, this is achieved by integrating your business and personal assets in a way that maximizes their ability to create wealth for you and your family. The ability to achieve this financial synergy is a key benefit of business ownership, which is why we call our approach *Smart Assets*. We believe these strategies can be invaluable to you as you seek to create and implement your most important financial plans. (Naturally, you will need to have your own lawyer and accountant review the strategies revealed in this book to make certain they are appropriate for your particular needs and circumstances.)

Smart Assets reveals a wealth of opportunities for the self-employed, but the book does not stop there. Many of the strategies outlined here can be highly valuable to corporate executives who have the resources and the determination to build and protect their wealth the smart way.

Each chapter of the book is designed to address critical components of an integrated plan designed to build and protect personal assets. As a preview of the wealth of ideas and strategies that await you on the following pages, let's see why each chapter represents an important part of the wealth creation process:

1. It is said that if you don't know where you are going, any road will get you there. Creating a plan serves as the foundation for a goal-oriented, wealth-building process.

2. Using leverage to accomplish your goals is always a smart strategy. We explain how to utilize the built-in tax advantages of planning opportunities that can serve as the bedrock of your finances. This area is ripe with opportunity for business owners who learn (as we will demonstrate throughout this book) how to integrate business and personal finances.

3. All too many people think of compensation exclusively in terms of salary. By learning how to go beyond this by tapping the power of fringe benefits, financial synergy can be achieved. Here, too, there are substantial opportunities for integrating business and personal finances.

   Paraphrasing Ben Franklin, it's not how much you make that counts, but how much you keep. In *Smart Assets,* we go a step further, making the case that if you want to build wealth, you will have to wisely invest what you keep. We offer a number of important guidelines.

4. Asset protection is a cornerstone of a sound financial strategy of wealth creation—and nothing is more effective in providing this protection than the appropriate life insurance. But here too, *Smart Assets* goes beyond the basics, revealing smart ways to fully tap the value

of life insurance by utilizing a number of highly effective insurance-related financial strategies.

5. Leverage can be a powerful element in a plan to build and protect wealth. Interestingly, a good deal of leverage—especially as it relates to minimizing taxes—can be achieved by shifting assets to family members. We offer a number of smart guidelines.

   All too often, successful people are so focused on building assets that they overlook the devastating impact of estate taxes, which can even force the sale of a family-owned business. We reveal smart ways to help plan for the future, avoid estate-tax meltdown, and continue to build personal wealth.

6. Estate taxes are an identifiable financial threat; others are unpredictable and potentially even more devastating. But *planning* can prove invaluable for virtually any scenario . . . and *Smart Assets* offers a range of strategies.

7. Business owners have an extraordinary opportunity to integrate business and personal finances. Because your business is often the most valuable asset and the most prodigious generator of personal wealth, we close with a number of ideas for keeping that asset alive and well and growing.

Smart Assets will reveal how you can

1. Establish a four-step financial blueprint for you and your family.

2. Save income taxes by shifting earned income from parents in high tax brackets to children in lower tax brackets.

3. Convert business equity into cash in a tax-favored way and simultaneously promote employee morale through employee stock ownership plans.

4. Reduce income taxes and increase personal wealth through qualified pension and profit-sharing plans.

5. Maximize the amount of money passing to beneficiaries in qualified retirement plans by purchasing life insurance on a tax-deductible basis.

6. Create tax-deductible life insurance programs and severance-pay benefit plans that favor key employees—that is, those you must retain for your business to grow.

7. Borrow money tax interest free from your corporation.

8. Protect your business by compensating key employees with restrictive benefit plans through "golden handcuffs."

9. Use corporate dollars to purchase permanent life insurance for key employees through split-dollar arrangements.

10. Provide discriminatory retirement benefits for employed family members and key employees through nonqualified deferred compensation arrangements.

11. Use life insurance and annuity products to accumulate money on a tax-favored basis to help pay for your children's education.

12. Keep control of property and assets and reduce or avoid estate taxes through family limited partnerships.

13. Provide permanent life insurance protection for your family in an efficient way by using group carve-out arrangements.

14. Assign more of your business by gift to family members with minimal or no gift-tax consequences by utilizing a discount for the transfer of a minority interest.

15. Reduce or avoid federal estate taxes and gift taxes by efficiently using trusts.

16. Learn how certain personal and business property can be protected from the claims of general creditors.

17. Learn how to protect your earned income from a covered illness or injury with disability income insurance.

18. Protect the value of your business with properly structured and properly funded buyout arrangements.

19. Avoid the capital gains tax by selling appreciated property inside a charitable remainder trust, and realize a tax deduction for the value of the charitable gift.

20. Learn creative business techniques to make your business grow and profit.

Clearly, every strategy will not be right for you. In fact, maybe only one or two will be precisely right at this time. So we recommend the following approach: As you read through *Smart Assets,* review the various ideas presented in the book— whether they are ways to minimize taxation now, protect your estate, or invest for the future—then select the ones you find most appealing and review them with your tax and financial professionals. You'll be on your way to putting *Smart Assets* to work for you.

George D. Brenner, JD, CLU, ChFC
John T. Cecere, CLU
Stanfield Hill, JD, CLU
Barry L. Rabinovich, JD, AEP

CONTENTS

Chapter 4

Chapter 5

Chapter 6

Chapter 7

Protecting Your Assets: Avoid the Worst Case . . . By Planning for It   147

Chapter 8

Growing Your Business   165

1

It All Starts with a Plan

Key Concepts Revealed in This Chapter

The Ultimate Synergy
Utilizing S Corporations, Limited Liability
  Companies, and Family Limited Partnerships
Explore Gift Lease-Backs

Although different people have different financial circumstances and objectives, a common thread still links most: the goal of achieving financial independence by creating and protecting wealth. How can you assess your progress toward achieving this goal? Take this simple test: Note how much you earn and the amount of your liquid assets. Next apply this simple mathematical formula: If the total of the earnings from your assets multiplied by a reasonable interest factor of 6 percent (or the prevailing rate) equals or surpasses your current earnings, you may have achieved financial independence. Whether you pass this test or not, you may want to increase your wealth, depending on changing objectives and economic environment.

How will you accomplish your goal of financial independence? The wisest route is to utilize the financial strategies developed by experts in the fields of tax, investment, financial, and estate and business planning—strategies that, in great part, enable you to *integrate* your business and personal financial goals, and build assets in the process. We call this approach *Smart Assets*.

As with every financial strategy, ours requires that you begin with a blueprint for managing your money—specifically, how you make it, accumulate it, grow it, distribute it, and preserve it. This can never be based on a generic approach. Instead, it must reflect your resources, lifestyle, priorities, and willingness to be open to new ideas and take some risk.

With this in mind, consider the following key steps in creating a Smart Assets blueprint.

Four-Step Process

1. Determine your objectives.

Where do you want to be, financially, in 5, 10, or 20 years? How much money will it take to support your ideal lifestyle? These goals, in whatever form they take, should be viewed as financial targets; they are critical because they provide quantifiable goals and the motivation to achieve them.

With this in mind, create a list of your financial needs and objectives for each decade of your life expectancy, and project the costs to meet those needs. (Be sure to factor in inflation.)

This will place your targets in a real-world dollars and cents framework and give you something specific to shoot for.

2. Establish your baseline.

The second step in financial planning is to determine where you are financially today. This is important because it allows you to determine how far you have to go to get where you want. With this in mind, you'll need to analyze your current financial position, taking stock of assets, income, and taxes. The best approach is to create a personal asset inventory by listing all your business and personal assets and assigning dollar figures to them. Equally important, you must develop a personal net worth statement, which lists your assets and liabilities, subtracts the former from the latter, and reveals how much real wealth you have today.

3. Create a road map.

This is simply a strategy for getting where you want to go. It should encompass Smart Assets tactics designed to harness the synergies of your business and personal assets and turn them into wealth-producing machines. Your road map is best developed by identifying the strategies in this book most appropriate for your goals and circumstances and working with your advisors (including lawyers, accountants, and insurance professionals) to link them into an integrated plan.

4. Monitor and update.

After embarking on your plan, review and modify it every year so that it stays consistent with life's major financial changes (business events, marital status, tax legislation, etc.). And bear in mind, it is important to monitor and update objectives as well as results because each affects the other.

THE ULTIMATE SYNERGY

As business owners you have an unusual opportunity to integrate the power of your business and personal assets. This is a cornerstone of the Smart Assets approach. When this integration is performed properly, you can achieve significant synergy.

For an example of how this can work, and the financial power it delivers, let's take a look at so-called *income-shifting strategies*. Income shifting is the transfer or shifting of income by one family member to another, who is usually in a lower tax bracket.

Business owners have an unusual opportunity to integrate the power of business and personal assets.

Assume, for example, that Paul Phillips owns a successful wholesale jewelry operation, ABC Jewelry. Paul's earnings from ABC, along with other investment income, put him within the top federal tax bracket— 39.6 percent. Paul's two children— Kate, age 13, and Tony, age 16—work part-time at ABC after school and on weekends, doing office chores such as filling orders and straightening up the stock. Based on the children's abilities and the time they spend on the job, Paul pays Kate $3,700 in wages, and Tony gets $6,300, for a total of $10,000 for 1995. The first $3,900 of 1995 annual income, adjusted annually for inflation, is tax free to the children, and, generally, Paul can still keep his dependency exemptions.

Here's where one of the benefits of integrating business and personal financial strategies comes in to play. If Paul pays the tax on that $10,000, he would have to pay $3,900 to the federal government. Partly because his children are in lower tax brackets, Paul could save up to $1,500 per child per year in taxes. And the children can use the money they make working at ABC for expenses they would otherwise expect their parents to pay.

As a sweetener, ABC can deduct the paychecks it gives to the children (providing it treats them no differently than any other full- or part-time employee) because the compensation represents reasonable wages for work actually performed. To establish this, Paul should keep a record of the hours the children work, the rate per hour, and the payment dates. If the business is unincorporated, no Social Security or unemployment tax need be withheld (if the child is under 18).

If you think that hiring children to work in your business becomes practical only if they are of high school age or older, you are likely shortchanging yourself. Depending on your children's ability, age, and motivation, you can even put grade schoolers to work. Consider these real-world income-shifting strategies:

- A real estate and trailer park owner pays his three children (ages 7 to 12) to perform such tasks as grounds maintenance, reading of electric and gas meters, mopping and cleaning, and delivering leaflets to tenants.
- A physician's two children (ages 13 and 15) work in his home office, answering the telephone and working on insurance forms and patient bills.

Finally, most or all of the earnings—which can be thought of as a tax-deductible allowance—can be kept in a custodial account for the children until they reach the age of majority (which is age 18 or 21, depending on your state of residence). This means parents can oversee the funds, making sure that the money is saved or invested rather than being squandered by the children as soon as it is earned. There is no downside to using this strategy. Probably, the worst that could happen is that the Internal Revenue Service (IRS) could view the children's earnings as excessive or not reasonable and tax them to the parent, as before.

UTILIZING S CORPORATIONS, LIMITED LIABILITY COMPANIES, AND FAMILY LIMITED PARTNERSHIPS

Here's another way to accomplish income shifting without putting your children to work. To accomplish this, you have to run your business (or elect to do so) as an S corporation, a limited liability company, or a family limited partnership. As a bit of background, net earnings generated by S corporations (after reasonable salaries) are taxable to its shareholders pro rata, based on their percentage share of ownership. This is true whether or not these earnings are actually distributed out of the company. The net earnings of a limited liability company or limited partnership can be distributed in the same manner, by prior agreement.

Returning to our earlier example, assume ABC is an S corporation and Paul gifted 49 percent of his stock to his children

(Kate and Tony). The gift was accomplished over sufficient time so that no gift tax was due. Given this scenario, 49 percent of the company's net earnings would be taxed to the children, even if they are not employees. (If the children are minors, their stock could actually be given to qualified S corporation trusts created for the benefit of each child.) Here again, the lower bracket tax savings may come into play, with the children's share of the earnings taxed at 15 percent as opposed to Paul's 39 percent. Clearly, more of the income generated by the business stays in the family and, if properly invested, can be used to create even more income. (Here, too, an additional sweetener comes into play: Under Revenue Ruling 93-12, gifts of a minority interest in a family business are eligible for a discount for gift-tax valuation purposes!

EXPLORE GIFT LEASE-BACKS

Do you want another way to shift income? Business equipment or real estate can be gifted to low-tax-bracket family members (generally children) and then leased to the high-bracket business entity (that is, a family partnership, sole proprietorship, S corporation, or professional service C corporation).

It works this way: Reasonable lease payments could provide the business with a 34 percent income tax deduction, but the payments might be taxed to the children at a 15 percent rate. Like the previous idea, this would result only if the "kiddie tax" did not apply (i.e., the children are at least 14). The resulting net tax savings is about 20 percent on each lease payment. What's more, the lease payment, as well as the business property, could be removed from the parents' estate for estate-tax purposes, but only if the gifts qualified for the $10,000 annual gift-tax exclusion.

As you can see from these relatively simple examples, with Smart Assets strategies, you can unleash the full power of your business and personal finances.

Smart Plans to Boost Employee Morale, Reduce Taxes, and Build Wealth

Key Concepts Revealed in This Chapter

Employee Stock Ownership Plans
Pension Plan Options at a Glance
Accumulating Wealth outside the Business
401(k) Plans
Insurance Strategy
The Appeal of Simplified Employee Pension Plans
SEPs and Profit Sharing: A Comparison
Putting Retirement Funds to Work Now: Turn
  Retirement Funds into Working Capital without a
  Penalty
Summary

To this point, we have focused on the foundation of our Smart Assets strategy: If you are wise, you will integrate your business and personal finances, creating a synergy that serves as a catalyst for the wealth-building process. With this in mind, take this quiz:

As the owner of a closely held business, your primary goal is to

- Keep growing the company.
- Raise the limit on productivity.
- Gain a powerful competitive advantage.
- Build your personal wealth.

Time's up: Your answer please.

It's not that easy, you say. If you claim that *all* of the objectives are critical, there's no arguing with you. But when you think about it, only one—*building your wealth*—should rank at the top of the list. Why do we say this? Simply because all the effort you put into growing your company, raising productivity, and battling the competition are not ends unto themselves. Instead, they are means to an end, designed to build wealth for yourself and your family. That's the real payoff for entrepreneurial success. At least it should be.

Let's step back for a moment and put things in perspective. Chapter 1 briefly reviewed a number of tax-wise ways to integrate business and personal finances . . . all with the goal of building wealth. The time has come to explore this concept further. Specifically, let's review how you can utilize smart, tax-wise plans designed to raise employee morale and simultaneously build your personal assets.

Here's how you can get started employing Smart Assets strategies in your business: Assume you've set out to raise your company's employee morale. Although you may be experimenting with a number of traditional approaches—such as awarding bonuses and empowering people to make a wider range of decisions—you can also utilize a more creative approach, one that effectively integrates your business and personal finances by enabling you to raise morale while simultaneously turning a substantial portion of your sweat equity into cash.

Entirely disparate goals? So one would think. But by utilizing the Smart Assets approach, you can accomplish this two-for-one strategy, enriching the payoff across the board.

EMPLOYEE STOCK OWNERSHIP PLANS

Achieving your dual goal can be made possible through the use of an employee stock ownership plan (ESOP), which is a type of qualified defined contribution retirement plan that enables employees to gain equity in the business. It works this way: As the employer, your corporation makes contributions to an ESOP trust fund (your lawyer can set one up) that is administered for the benefit of participating employees. Income earned by the ESOP trust is tax deferred, corporate contributions made to the ESOP trust on behalf of employees are tax deductible, and income tax is not paid by employees until they actually receive funds from the plan.

A major distinction between ESOPs and other pension and profit-sharing plans is that ESOPs are designed to allow the qualified plans to own the stock of the sponsoring corporation. When the stock is contributed to the ESOP, the corporation gets a full income tax deduction, just as if the contribution had been made in cash.

This can have an immediate positive impact on the corporation's financial position. Here's why: If a regular C corporation (an S corporation generally cannot have an ESOP) is in a 40 percent combined state and federal income tax bracket and makes a tax-deductible $100,000 cash contribution to its profit-sharing plan, it will *decrease* its working capital and cash flow by $60,000. However, a corresponding $100,000 contribution to an ESOP trust of corporate stock *increases* the corporation's working capital and cash flow by $40,000 because the business receives a $100,000 deduction without putting out any cash. That's a financial "swing" of $100,000!

A Market for Shares

In addition to providing this benefit to the corporation, the ESOP delivers a potential windfall for the business owner by creating a market for the shares of the closely held business because an ESOP can acquire corporate stock by purchasing it from major shareholders. Funds to pay for the stock can be borrowed by the ESOP from banks, insurance companies, regulated investment companies, and certain other lending institutions, and the loan is secured by a guarantee from the company. The ESOP repays the loan by using the annual tax-deductible cash contributions made to it by the corporation, or by future dividends paid on the corporate stock (which are also tax deductible).

Here's where the Smart Assets wealth-building feature comes into play. As a business owner, it is possible to sell your stock to the ESOP for cash, thus turning your sweat equity into cash. The loan to pay for your shares can once again be repaid by the corporation's tax-deductible dividends or cash contributions made to the ESOP (see Figure 2–1).

Even better, as the company's shareholder, under certain circumstances, the capital gain from the sale of your stock to the ESOP can be deferred under the tax-free exchange provisions in the Internal Revenue Code, Sec. 1042. This strategy provides a means for you to exchange your closely held stock for new stock, without currently being taxed at the time of the gain. Only upon the subsequent sale of the new stock will gain be recognized (if any) to the extent that gain was not recognized at the time the new stock was acquired. This can also be used as a business expansion technique. Under this strategy, it is possible to capitalize a new venture with the tax-deferred profits realized from the sale of stock to the ESOP.

To qualify for this powerful tax advantage, the following requirements must be met:

- The ESOP must own, after the sale, at least 30 percent of all the company's outstanding stock.
- As the selling shareholder, you must have held the stock for at least three years.
- You must reinvest the gains from the sale of your stock (within a specific replacement period) in "qualified replacement property," which includes stocks and bonds of certain U.S. operating corporations.

Other conditions may also apply.

FIGURE 2–1

How to Create a Market for Shares of Your Closely Held Business

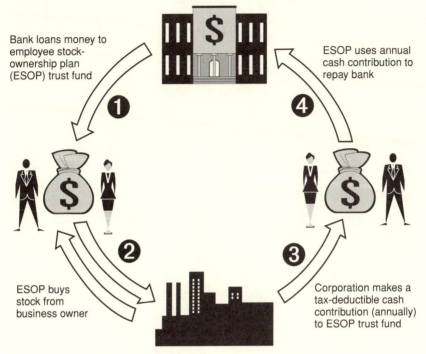

Source: *Profit Magazine*, May/June 1994, pp. 40–50.

The bottom line is that by selling part of your company to an ESOP, you can diversify your personal business stock holdings into more traditional investments and, at the same time, defer tax on capital gains. You can also offer your employees an equity stake in your company—which goes a long way toward building a high level of morale.

ESOP Example

Business owner Smith wants to achieve greater asset diversification. Currently, her portfolio consists of $500,000 of publicly traded stock and $2,500,000 of closely held company stock. The company's profit-sharing plan has a total value of $500,000.

Assume Smith wants to sell 30 percent of her company's stock and reinvest the proceeds in publicly traded securities. Through the use of an ESOP, Smith could sell $750,000 of stock free of current capital gains tax and, at the same time, fund employee retirement benefits. The process might work this way:

> By selling part of your company to an ESOP, you can diversify your personal business stock holdings into more traditional investments and defer tax on capital gains.

1. The corporation converts its profit-sharing plan to an ESOP.

2. The ESOP borrows $500,000 from a bank, adds $250,000 from the former profit-sharing plan, and buys $750,000 of stock from the business owner. In effect, the employees of the company are buying (through the ESOP) 30 percent of the company from Smith, providing her with $750,000 of liquidity, which can be reinvested.

3. No later than 12 months after the sale, Smith reinvests the cash proceeds in qualified replacement securities. (No capital gains taxes are due until the replacement securities are sold.) Smith now owns a more diversified portfolio consisting of $1,250,000 of publicly traded stock and $1,750,000 of closely held stock.

Smart Strategy

Bear in mind that participating employees can require the corporation to repurchase the corporate shares distributed by the ESOP to them at retirement, according to a fair valuation formula. This repurchase provision is important to employees, who want the assurance that, in the case of disability, employment termination, retirement, or death, there will be a ready buyer to purchase their stock if the company is not publicly traded. This is undesirable, though, because it creates an obligation for the ESOP and the company. To honor the repurchase agreement, the company will need sufficient cash to buy back the employees' stock from either the ESOP or the employee.

Selecting a funding program to cope with this repurchase liability is a key long-range planning issue. In many cases, the purchase of corporate-owned life insurance can provide a viable solution because it creates a pool of money that can be used to buy the shares and provide the employee benefit.

Clearly, an ESOP can be a win/win strategy for closely held companies, helping to build the wealth of the business and the wealth of their owners. Here's why: Corporate profits increase when workers are more productive, and workers are more productive when they have a financial stake in the success of their employer. The ESOP offers you, the business owner, the opportunity to cash out all or part of your business equity conveniently and profitably, especially when no buyer or successor exists for your business.

As this Smart Assets strategy demonstrates, when business and personal finances are properly integrated, a small company can be more than a cash flow generator. It can be a wealth builder.

Time for a quick summary of what we have learned to this point: Protecting and preserving a closely held business as it evolves is only one of the critical components of successful management. More important is to build the owner's assets in tandem with the growth of the business, capitalizing on this success to amass personal wealth over the years.

Qualified retirement plans can serve as excellent vehicles for accomplishing this. Put simply, these enable you to invest in wealth-building programs with pre-tax dollars and to have those dollars compound over the years on a tax-deferred basis.

PENSION PLAN OPTIONS AT A GLANCE

There was a time when mention of the words *pension plan* brought to mind an image of a retirement fund that cost an employer money. But today's pension and profit-sharing plans can be, first and foremost, tax-planning tools for business owners. They can save money—some of which would otherwise be paid in taxes.

A qualified pension or profit-sharing plan meets certain requirements in the Internal Revenue Code that make it eligible for special tax treatment. These plans can be used by self-employed individuals, partnerships, organizations, associations, or corporations.

The Cost of Doing Nothing

A profitable business that fails to take advantage of a qualified pension or profit-sharing plan for sheltering business earnings is probably losing an unnecessarily large portion of its hard-earned dollars to taxes. If the business merely retains earnings or distributes them out as dividends, salaries, or bonuses, corporate and personal income taxes severely erode their value. For example,

- Retained earnings of $37,500 would be reduced to $24,375 after corporate income tax is paid.
- Dividends paid from $37,500 in corporate earnings would be reduced to $9,375 after corporate and personal income taxes are paid.
- A salary increase or bonus of $37,500 would be worth only $22,500 after payment of personal income tax. (This example assumes a 35 percent corporate income tax rate and a 40 percent personal income tax rate.)

Pension plans are commonly thought of as the most effective way to accumulate wealth.

The Cost of Doing Something

The dollars a business contributes to its qualified pension or profit-sharing plan are tax deductible to the business; participants pay no current personal income tax on them either. And, while it is true that employers generally make pension or profit-sharing contributions on behalf of employees as well as themselves as employees, plans can often be designed so that they favor business owners. In fact, retirement planning professionals estimate that 80 percent or more of a small business's qualified plan contributions are typically made for the benefit of the owner-employee.

Accordingly, if the $37,500 in earnings mentioned earlier were contributed to a qualified pension or profit-sharing plan, typically only about $7,500 (20 percent) of that contribution would be on behalf of the rank-and-file employees because of their total salary. That would leave $30,000 directed toward the business owner's own retirement plan account. This is significantly more than the after-tax amount available to a business owner if a qualified plan were not used.

Essentially, the contributions on behalf of employees can be paid for with some of the dollars that would have otherwise been paid in taxes. The rest of the dollars that would have been paid in taxes go to the business owner's pension account to accumulate for his or her retirement.

ACCUMULATING WEALTH OUTSIDE THE BUSINESS

When a business owner accumulates dollars in a pension or profit-sharing plan, that accumulated wealth is separate from the business and business assets. When it comes time to retire, the business owner can access that wealth without having to sell or otherwise liquidate the assets of the business. They can pass on their business intact or, if they choose, sell it when they can optimize their profit. In addition to creating financial security, the pension or profit-sharing plan can improve the business. The plan can be structured to favor not only the owners but key employees as well. In that way, the owners can gain the loyalty of the key workers, and the continuity of the company's management can be supported. Moreover, the plan's employee benefits can foster goodwill and reduce employee turnover among rank-and-file employees. Employers can save tax dollars today . . . and build them faster for tomorrow.

> Once a business establishes a qualified pension or profit-sharing plan, the owner will benefit in three ways: tax savings, tax-deferred growth, and tax-favored distributions.

Once the business establishes a qualified pension or profit-sharing plan, the business owner will benefit from its tax advantages in significant ways. By providing annual tax savings and tax-deferred growth all during their business life and tax-favored distributions when they retire, the plan enables the business owner to accumulate more dollars faster.

Phase 1: Annual Tax Savings from Income Tax Deductions

Each time the business makes a contribution to its qualified pension or profit-sharing plan, it is immediately tax deductible to the company. Furthermore, no current personal income tax is payable on any of the contributions. This favorable tax treatment results in considerable income tax savings.

Using the example discussed earlier, here's a comparison of what would happen if $37,500 of earnings was taken out of the business in three different ways—as corporate dividends, as a salary increase or bonus, or by contributing the earnings to a qualified plan. The comparison shows how much of the $37,500 could go to work for the business owner—and how much for the government—in each case.

Dividend		*Salary or Bonus*		*Qualified Plan*	
Corporate income tax	$13,125				
Personal income tax	$ 9,750	Personal income tax	$15,000	Contributions for employees	$ 7,500
Available to owner	$14,625	Available to owner	$22,500	Available to owner	$30,000
Dividends from $37,500 in corporate earnings		$37,500 salary increase or bonus		$37,500 qualified pension or profit-sharing plan contribution	

(This example assumes a 35 percent corporate tax rate and a 40 percent personal tax rate.)

Phase 2: Accelerated Growth of Assets through Tax Deferral

Once the plan's tax savings have preserved more of the annual business earnings for investment, the plan's tax deferral takes over and accelerates the growth of wealth. All plan earnings

FIGURE 2–2

Growth Comparison: Qualified Plan versus Dividends and Salary

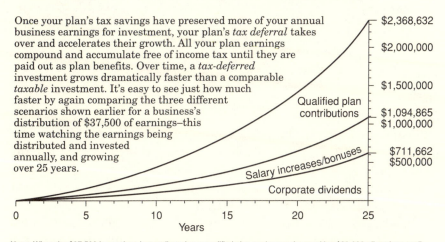

Once your plan's tax savings have preserved more of your annual business earnings for investment, your plan's *tax deferral* takes over and accelerates their growth. All your plan earnings compound and accumulate free of income tax until they are paid out as plan benefits. Over time, a *tax-deferred* investment grows dramatically faster than a comparable *taxable* investment. It's easy to see just how much faster by again comparing the three different scenarios shown earlier for a business's distribution of $37,500 of earnings–this time watching the earnings being distributed and invested annually, and growing over 25 years.

$2,368,632
$2,000,000
$1,500,000

Qualified plan contributions

$1,094,865
$1,000,000

Salary increases/bonuses

$711,662
$500,000

Corporate dividends

Years: 0   5   10   15   20   25

Note: When the $37,500 in earnings is contributed to a qualified plan each year, the resulting $30,000 allocations available to the owner grow tax-deferred. This tax-deferred growth-is considerably faster than the growth of the $14,625 after-tax dividends or the $22,500 after-tax salary/bonuses, which earn the same rate of return–8 percent–but do not benefit from tax deferral. (The after-tax comparison is shown in table 2–1 on page 18).

    This example assumes an 8 percent pre-tax yield for all three scenarios, a 35 percent corporate tax rate, and a 40 percent personal tax rate.

compound and accumulate free of income tax until they are paid out as plan benefits. Over time, a tax-deferred investment grows dramatically faster than a comparable taxable investment (see Figure 2–2).

Phase 3: More Income for Your Retirement through Tax-Favored Distributions

When the business owner accesses the plan dollars, they continue to benefit from tax-favored treatment. Owners may elect to receive their accumulated benefits as a lump sum. Assuming they will be at least 59½ years old and will have participated in the plan for at least five years, they will have the advantage of "averaging" the distribution over five years for tax purposes, which can lower their overall tax. "Five-Year Averaging" is available until December 31, 1999. (Distributions may begin as late as April 1 following the calendar year in which a participant who is a "5% Owner" attains age 70½.) Owners also have the option of receiving regular fixed payments over a set period

TABLE 2–1

After-Tax Distribution: Qualified Plan versus Dividends and Salary after 25 Years

Corporate dividends	$ 711,662
Salary increases/bonuses	$1,094,865
Qualified plan	$1,515,407

of time or over the joint lifetime of them and their spouses. Income taxes are due only on the amount received each tax year. As a result of this continuing preferential tax treatment, the qualified plan maximizes the dollars available to the business owner at retirement (see Table 2–1).

After 25 years, the after-tax distribution from the qualified plan to the business owner is considerably greater than the accumulation available from either of the other two scenarios—the invested dividends or the invested salary increases or bonuses. (This example assumes that the owner takes a lump sum distribution from the qualified plan and uses five-year averaging for tax purposes, which is available until December 31, 1999). A 40 percent personal tax bracket is assumed.

Let's review some of the key types of qualified retirement plans:

1. Conventional profit-sharing plans offer the advant age of allowing for flexible contributions (made on a tax-deductible basis) that can vary year by year from 0 to 15 percent of the total payroll for all plan participants. Once contributions are made, they are allocated according to a formula based on pay levels. An effective customization technique, known as "Permitted Disparity," or "Social Security integration," may allow for contributions to be allocated in a way that provides an additional sum to employees earning more than the Social Security wage base. This, in effect, may permit entrepreneurs to steer a higher percentage of the plan benefits to themselves and key employees.

These plans generally favor younger business owners and managers who have many years to accumulate
savings for retirement.

2. Age-based profit-sharing plans, a relatively new concept, offer the same flexibility as conventional profit-
sharing plans with the distinction that contributions
are based on age as well as pay. Age-based plans dramatically favor older, higher-paid employees, which
usually include the business owner and key employees.
The ability to skew benefits to the owner and the oldest
key employee(s) has made age-based plans an immediate hit with business owners nationwide.

3. Money purchase plans can be attractive because they
permit a relatively large deductible contribution of up
to 25 percent of the total payroll of all plan participants.
Because they require a more even distribution across
the board, the plans are often a good choice for businesses with young owners and key employees who have
many years to accumulate savings for retirement and
who want to provide contributions in excess of 15 percent. Money purchase plans require fixed contributions
each year and limit annual allocations to individual
participants to 25 percent of earnings up to a maximum
of $30,000.

4. Defined benefit plans provide for a specific benefit at
retirement, which may be up to 100 percent of pay to
a maximum annual sum ($120,000 per year as of 1995).
Contributions are determined by the amount of money
required to fund the defined benefit. The plans are popular in very small (fewer than five employees) companies seeking to make large tax-deductible contributions
on behalf of older principals. With defined benefit
plans, the benefit formula first determines how large a
retirement benefit an employee is eligible to receive,
and then plan actuaries annually calculate the contribution required to achieve it.

Consider, a 54-year-old business owner who plans to retire at 65, currently earns $200,000 a year and has a 25-year old employee earning $25,000. The company can contribute about $56,000 to the defined benefit plan, 99 percent of which goes to the owner. Because benefits are guaranteed, the employer contributions must be adequate to pay pension benefits.

5. Target benefit plans are hybrids, combining some of the features of money purchase plans with some of the features of defined benefit plans. Contributions are fixed and may be as high as 25 percent of total pay of all plan participants. The plan formula specifies a benefit at retirement, which is targeted by the plan. Each participant's actual benefit is determined by contributions and earnings in their account, which may be greater than, equal to, or less than the targeted benefit.

Consider this example of an age-based plan: LMK Corporation is owned by Ms. Owner, age 45, who earns $150,000 annually and employs Ms. Employee, age 29, and Mr. Worker, age 24, who earn $35,000 and $25,000, respectively. Ms. Owner would like to establish a qualified plan that enables her to make flexible contributions annually and maximize her own plan allocation, while minimizing contributions on behalf of Ms. Employee and Mr. Worker.

Based on Ms. Owner's objectives, her age, the age of her two employees, and the amount of their annual compensation, it is determined that LMK Corporation should establish an age-based profit-sharing plan. In the current year, Ms. Owner wants LMK to make a plan contribution that will enable her to receive the maximum allowable allocation (that is, 25 percent of her annual compensation, up to $30,000). Based on Ms. Owner's objective, the plan's formula and design, and other factors that go into the calculation, it is determined that Ms. Owner's company will contribute a total of $31,500—$28,812 will be allocated to Ms. Owner and $2,688 to her two employees.

Ms. Owner had considered establishing a conventional profit-sharing plan. But, because she is considerably older than her employees, the age-based profit-sharing option proves to be more beneficial. The same $31,500 contribution to a conventional

FIGURE 2–3

Contributions

Conventional Profit-Sharing Plan

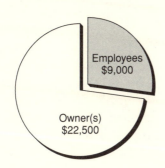

Employees
$9,000

Owner(s)
$22,500

Age-Based Profit-Sharing Plan

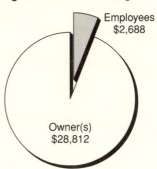

Employees
$2,688

Owner(s)
$28,812

profit-sharing plan would provide only $22,500 for Ms. Owner and $9,000 to her employees. The bottom line is that selecting the age-based approach resulted in a $6,312 difference in favor of Ms. Owner (see Figure 2–3).

The age-based profit-sharing plan also provides substantial tax benefits through retirement. Let's see how this unfolds.

The Immediate Benefit: Annual Tax Savings

The $31,500 LMK Corporation contributes to the age-based profit-sharing plan is tax deductible, saving the company $11,025 in corporate income tax. What's more, Ms. Owner does not pay personal income tax on the contribution. This puts considerably more dollars at Ms. Owner's disposal ($28,812) than would be possible by leaving the $31,500 in her company as retained earnings or by using it to pay herself a salary increase, bonus, or dividend—all of which are subject to corporate or personal income taxes.

The Ongoing Benefit: Accelerated Growth of Assets through Tax-Deferred Compounding

If Ms. Owner receives a $28,812 allocation each year, the plan may achieve an 8 percent annual yield, and the plan earnings will compound and accumulate free of income tax until they are distributed in 20 years. Over that time, a total of $1,423,973 will accumulate in Ms. Owner's account.

The Ultimate Benefit: More Income for Retirement through Tax-Favored Distributions

At the end of 20 years, Ms. Owner retires and LMK Corporation distributes to her the $1,423,973 age-based profit-sharing plan accumulation in a lump-sum payment. (Other payment options are available, including a monthly income stream for life.) Although this distribution is subject to personal income tax, Ms. Owner is entitled (until December 31, 1999) to use a special tax technique known as five-year averaging to reduce the amount of income taxes due (because she is over age 59½ and has participated in the plan for more than five years).

> By using matching, profit-sharing or other optional types of contributions, a 401(k) plan can be created that meets the company's specific business needs.

In the final tally, Ms. Owner will have amassed an after-tax nest egg of about $996,781. The integration of business and personal finances—the core of Smart Assets—has made it happen.

401(K) PLANS

At this point, let's discuss another retirement option, the 401(k) plan. A 401(k) plan enjoys all the same tax advantages of other tax-qualified retirement plans. But unlike other plans where all the costs are borne by the employer alone, the 401(k) can be funded with contributions made by the employees, through so-called *salary deferrals*. In fact, some 401(k) plans are designed so that they are funded by employee salary deferrals only, with no contributions from the employer. With employees partially or fully funding the plan themselves, the company's out-of-pocket costs can be kept to a minimum.

Flexibility in Design

A 401(k) plan gives companies a great variety of choices in plan design—without a fixed commitment. While the plan can be set up exclusively with employee salary deferrals, there are a number of ways in which the company can add contributions to enhance the employees' retirement benefits and encourage their participation in the plan.

The company can make "matching" contributions that partially or fully match each employee's salary deferral. The plan can also be designed with "profit-sharing" contributions that are discretionary from year to year. By using matching, profit-sharing or other optional types of contributions, a 401(k) plan can be created that meets the company's specific business needs.

Tax Advantages for the Business Owner and the Company

All contributions to the plan—salary deferrals as well as employer contributions—are tax deductible for the company. Each year, the total deductions for contributions are allowed to equal as much as 15 percent of the payroll for all participating employees, producing significant tax savings for the company.

And remember, since business owners are employees too, they can participate in the plan and benefit from the same tax-advantaged savings and growth opportunities enjoyed by all other participating employees.

Case Study: A 401(K) Plan in Action

The following case study illustrates how three owners of a hypothetical company can establish a 401(k) plan that cost effectively achieves their business objectives and personal financial goals. Table 2–2 helps set the scene.

The Primary Benefit: Employee Goodwill and Productivity

The three owners of SMS Corporation have decided to establish a 401(k) plan, primarily to stay competitive in the labor market. They feel the benefits of a 401(k) will help them continue to attract higher quality employees, reduce costly employee turnover, and, consequently, provide better customer service.

Secondary Benefit: Tax-Advantaged Savings for the Owners

Of secondary importance is the fact that the three owners will also be able to take advantage of the 401(k) plan to augment

TABLE 2–2

The Company: SMS Corporation

The Owners

Mr. Stephens	Ms. Marin	Mr. Sherman
Age 43	Age 38	Age 41
Annual salary $150,000	Annual salary $150,000	Annual salary $150,000

Other Employees

Twenty-two, with annual salaries ranging from $13,000 to $48,000
Total payroll for other employees is $621,534

their own individual retirement savings. Their objective is to use the plan to defer as much of their salaries as is permitted by law up to 20 percent of gross salary.

The Incentive to Employees: Matching Contributions

In a 401(k) plan, the amount an owner or executive may save is determined by how much the rank-and-file employees defer from their salaries. In this case, for the owners to ensure that they will be able to defer approximately 6.2 percent of their salaries, it is necessary that the average deferral of all the other employees be at least 4.2 percent of salary. As an incentive to achieve this level of employee participation, the owners have decided to offer matching contributions of $0.50 for every dollar of employee deferrals up to 5 percent of salary.

The Owners' Personal Accumulation Potential

In addition to a $9,240 deferral, the three owners will also each receive a matching contribution of $3,750 from the company (half of 5 percent of their salary), giving them each a total contribution to their personal 401(k) account of $12,990 for the year. Based on each of their ages and assuming a 7 percent annual rate of return on their savings, their annual 401(k) savings are projected to grow to about $681,145 for Mr. Stephens, $1,035,273 for Ms. Marin, and $808,615 for Mr. Sherman by the time each reaches age 65.

The Net Cost to the Company

If the owners and employees participate as discussed, SMS Corporation's total contribution to the plan would be $85,585, which includes the entire amount of salary deferrals made by the owners and other employees plus all matching contributions made by the company. Since all salary deferrals represent money that the company would pay as salary anyway, the cost of the plan (apart from administrative expense) is limited to the after-tax cost of $21,430 in matching contributions, which is just $13,930.

Of this net after-tax outlay, $9,000 reflects the $3,000 matching contributions made on behalf of each of the three owners. So, the bottom-line cost of the plan is only $4,930 in terms of money the company contributes that does not come back to the owners in the form of corporate tax savings or deposits to their individual 401(k) accounts.

401(k) Plan Summary

- Annual maximum employer contributions: 15 percent of participating payroll (employee deferrals count toward the 15 percent maximum).

- Pre-tax employee salary deferrals: (*a*) Annual maximum: 20 percent of individual participant's gross compensation, up to $9,240 (as indexed for 1995). (*b*) Deferrals by highly compensated employees are subject to nondiscrimination test. (*c*) After-tax contributions are also possible.

- Individual participant allocations: A combination of employer contributions on behalf of each individual participant and the participant's salary deferrals.

- Annual maximum: 25 percent of individual participant's net compensation up to $30,000.

- Integrated with Social Security: Available for employer's discretionary profit-sharing contributions only.

- Employee investment discretion: Participants select investments from options offered by trustee.

INSURANCE STRATEGY

A qualified retirement plan should offer a variety of options designed to meet the personal investment goals of the participants. Given the unpredictable nature of financial markets, one of these options should be conservative in nature and provide some type of guarantee. That's where life insurance can play an interesting role in funding the plan.

Until this point, you may not have thought of life insurance as an appropriate option for a qualified plan. But let's explore this issue. If there is a need for life insurance, why not satisfy that need with tax-deductible dollars? Considering that qualified plan contributions are made with pre-tax dollars, this can be a cost-effective way to acquire coverage. This means the business owner will have extra dollars to save, spend, or reinvest in the business, as illustrated in the accompanying example.

	Outside Plan	Inside Plan
Earnings	$1,000	$1,000
Taxes (35%)	350	0
Premium	650	650*
Balance for savings	$ 0	$ 350

*Premium must not violate incidental death benefit limits.

There are other cost-saving advantages and benefits as well. For example, buying insurance inside your qualified plan may be a significantly better choice than relying on group insurance alone. In most cases, the amount of group coverage available is not sufficient to meet individual insurance needs, and the cumulative cost of group insurance over many years can be quite expensive. Furthermore, group insurance may reduce or terminate at retirement, or be very expensive to convert, even if your insurance needs do not change.

Sound Funding Alternative

Life insurance in a qualified plan can provide values at retirement that can match those of conservative investments. Since it is prudent to include conservative investments as part of a qualified plan portfolio, allocating dollars toward life insurance that provides cash value which can be used for retirement and a death benefit for family income protection can be a smart strategy.

Increased Benefits for Your Beneficiaries

At retirement, insured plan participants receive the added benefit of a permanent life insurance policy they may take with them in addition to any amounts accumulated in the plan. At the time of a participant's death, whether he or she is still a plan participant or after retirement if the policy has been maintained, an added death benefit will be paid to beneficiaries, income tax free, over and above the cash accumulated on their behalf in the plan. The insurance benefit can be particularly beneficial to plan participants who become uninsurable at a later age and would not otherwise be able to purchase insurance when they need it (see Table 2–3).

> Life insurance in a qualified plan can provide values at retirement that can match those of conservative investments.

A qualified plan enables business owners to build wealth outside their business for their future. The funds can be used for the business owner's retirement, to enable him or her to pass on or sell the business intact, or to provide benefits for the family.

Unforeseen events, unfortunately, can undo even the most carefully constructed plan. A decline in investment performance or economic recession could make future plan contributions burdensome or impossible. Premature death or disability could halt the growth of the plan benefit before desired goals have been achieved. Life insurance in a plan can help protect the goals a business owner is working so hard to achieve.

Bear this in mind: Because the primary purpose of qualified plans is to provide retirement benefits, life insurance coverage must be "incidental," meaning the amount of insurance that may be purchased on each participant is limited. Generally, premiums must be less than 50 percent of the plan contributions for whole life and no more than 25 percent for term or universal life insurance is purchased.

TABLE 2–3

Plan Comparison

Retirement Plan without Insurance	Retirement Plan with Insurance	
	During Life	**At Death**
$1,776,474	$1,575,833[a]	$1,907,105[b]
Total benefit at age 65	plus pure life insurance protection, retirement benefit at age 65	Death benefit at age 65
Income taxes	Income Taxes	Income taxes
$606,684	$528,420	$528,420[c]
Benefit at retirement or death after taxes	Benefit at retirement after tax	Benefit at death after income Taxes
$1,169,790	$1,047,413 (plus life insurance protection)	$1,378,685

This illustration assumes a profit-sharing plan providing a 15 percent contribution annually for a participant earning $150,000 annually beginning at age 40 until retirement or death. An 8 percent pre-tax yield is assumed on all monies contributed to the plan and not applied to insurance. Life insurance illustrated is MONY Premier Plus-IQP, providing a death benefit of $364,078, nonsmoker, preferred rates with waiver of premium. Twenty-five percent of plan contributions are applied to pay life insurance premiums. Policy values are based on guaranteed cash values and the 1995 illustrative dividend scale; dividends are not guaranteed or estimates of future results. Taxes on distributions assume the participant takes a lump-sum distribution and uses five-year averaging. Personal tax brackets applied are those in effect for 1995. A 35 percent corporate tax bracket is assumed.

[a] This amount includes accumulated dividends that are not guaranteed. Benefits including guaranteed life insurance cash values are $1,125,926.

[b] This amount includes accumulated dividends that are not guaranteed. Benefits including guaranteed life insurance proceeds are $1,490,004.

[c] Amount of pure life insurance protection passes income tax free.

To recap, here's why allocating some of your plan contribution to life insurance can be financially savvy:

- When life insurance is built into a qualified plan, premiums are paid with pre-tax dollars. Compared with buying insurance outside of a plan, you get more coverage for the same expense.

- When life insurance is included in a qualified plan, your beneficiaries receive a substantial benefit whether you live to retirement or die prematurely.

- Taxable retirement benefit dollars can be transformed into nontaxable dollars.

- Life insurance contracts may be retained by participants after termination of employment at original premium rates, regardless of changes in health. In addition, if the individual becomes a participant in another qualified employer plan, life insurance policies may be rolled into that qualified plan without incurring a tax liability.

THE APPEAL OF SIMPLIFIED EMPLOYEE PENSION PLANS

Now let's take a look at a popular qualified employer plan alternative—the simplified employee pension plan (SEP). A SEP can be attractive to business owners because it requires lower startup costs and lesser ongoing maintenance fees when compared with other types of plans. With SEPs, employers may make discretionary contributions to employees' individual retirement accounts (IRAs), equal to the lesser of $22,500 or 15 percent of compensation for the applicable year.

The SEP plan must be established and contributions made by your company's tax filing deadline, plus extensions; the extended deadline for establishing SEPs is an advantage when compared with the usual December 31 deadline for profit-sharing money purchase plans and other qualified plans.

For those "eligible employers" who want an administratively simple tax-favored method of contributing to their employees' retirement, a SIMPLE plan (Savings Incentive Match Plan For Employees) may be an attractive option. A SIMPLE plan can be designed to look like an IRA or 401(k). Traditional "non-discrimination" rules and "top heavy plan" rules do not apply. Although "eligible employers" can have up to 100 employees, the SIMPLE plan is particularly suited for employers that have few employees and high plan administration costs.

SEPs AND PROFIT SHARING: A COMPARISON

While a SEP is easy to establish and monitor, it may be more simplistic than simplified for many businesses. A profit-sharing plan, although seemingly more expensive and cumbersome, can be reasonably easy and somewhat more cost effective than a SEP.

SEPs are attractive to business owners because they require lower startup costs and lesser ongoing maintenance fees.

For example, employees who participate in a SEP are fully vested in all sums allocated to them. This gives them less incentive to stay with the company. In contrast, employees usually must work five to seven years before becoming fully vested in a profit-sharing plan. Those who leave before this waiting period forfeit the invested dollars allocated to their accounts to that point. These sums may be reallocated to the remaining plan participants, including the business owner. Such reallocations must satisfy the nondiscrimination rules.

PUTTING RETIREMENT FUNDS TO WORK NOW: TURN RETIREMENT FUNDS INTO WORKING CAPITAL WITHOUT A PENALTY

People in the field of retirement planning offer two axioms: (*1*) "The best way to save is in a tax-qualified retirement plan." (*2*) "When it comes to retirement plans, too much of a good thing can prove to be a tax disaster." What happens when these two axioms collide? Let's take a closer look at this dichotomy.

Most Americans feel that they can never save too much for retirement. Based on this mindset, many business owners may actually be putting away too much money in tax-qualified retirement savings instead of using the cash during their lifetime to start a new company, expand an existing business, or provide income and financial protection for their families.

Consider this example: You and your spouse are age 50, and the current value of your profit-sharing plan is $1,000,000.

Your joint predicted mortality is age 85, and your funds are earning about 7 percent per year. As required by law, at age 70½ you start to withdraw the minimal amount from your plan annually, with the remaining funds continuing to grow at 7 percent.

If this continues to predicted mortality, the value of your plan at age 85 will be $2,113,053. But, at death, after deducting a potential 55 percent estate tax of $1,162,179 (you have a net worth over $3,000,000), and a 40 percent income tax of $380,350, your children may inherit as little as $570,524 from the profit-sharing plan. The percentage of your tax-qualified plan actually inherited by your children could be a mere 27 percent, with a whopping $1,542,529 lost to taxation. State income and death taxes may further increase this amount and leave even less for your children. On the other hand, if amounts are withdrawn from the plan before age 59½ to use in a business or to make gifts to your children, there normally will be a 10 percent penalty in addition to the regular income tax on amounts withdrawn. The 10 percent penalty tax is imposed under Internal Revenue Code Section 72(t).

Making Section 72(t) Work for You

You can avoid losing such a large amount to taxation as well as the 10 percent penalty tax by taking advantage of an under-utilized exception known as Section 72(t)(2)(A)(iv) of the Internal Revenue Code. Essentially, this exception allows people under the age of 59½ to annuitize IRAs, rollover IRAs, and eligible qualified plans without incurring the 10 percent penalty tax that would otherwise be applicable. To annuitize a plan means to begin receiving a series of substantially equal periodic payments from the plan over your life expectancy or over the joint life expectancy of you and your beneficiary.

By annuitizing payments from your qualified plan, or by terminating a qualified plan prior to age 59½ and rolling the money over into an IRA, which is then annuitized, you can effectively convert retirement funds into working capital that can be used to achieve business and personal financial goals without paying the 10 percent penalty tax. At the same time, you can replace part or all of the value of the qualified plan account with life insurance. However, the cost of the life insurance will reduce the amount of working capital. The insurance program can help protect your heirs from the decline in the value of your plan or your overall estate.

Here's a case in point: Using one of the three accepted annuitization methods, a 50-year-old business owner with a $250,000 rollover IRA should be able to generate a cash flow of about $1,784 per month without paying the 10 percent penalty tax. This amount is based on annuitizing the IRA account over life. Actual annuity rates can vary, depending on age, type of annuity, and interest rates. (Of course, income tax will still be due.) Once the owner reaches age 59½ (and has fully participated in the annuitization plan for at least five years), he or she can modify or even discontinue the monthly withdrawals if they are no longer needed. Then, plan assets can continue to accumulate on a tax-deferred basis. (Caveat: Strict rules must be followed in calculating and administering these IRA withdrawals.)

Consider these related strategies and benefits: The regular income tax levied on withdrawals may be offset by using some of the money to pay tax-deductible expenses, such as interest on a bank loan that is used in connection with a business. Part of the money can be used to purchase life insurance to help replace the assets used prior to retirement with an income-tax-free death benefit for your family.

Following the Rules

In general, this penalty avoidance strategy can be used for qualified retirement plans, including IRAs, with little or no restrictions. Let's explore additional smart plans that can accomplish business goals while building personal wealth.

Welfare Benefit Plans

As you know, qualified pension plans can help you meet retirement funding needs, provide valuable benefits to yourself and your employees, and offer income tax deductions for the company. What you might not know is that there is another option, a "welfare benefit plan," that also uses tax-deductible contributions. It can serve as a supplement to a qualified retirement plan by providing severance pay and life insurance benefits, although it cannot provide retirement benefits or deferred compensation.

Welfare benefit plans are particularly attractive to smaller businesses, in part because their funding costs can be skewed relatively easily, according to salary. Thus, highly paid business owners can be allocated the lion's share of the contributions, while the corporation can claim the entire cost as a tax deduction.

Here's how such plans could work: The company joins an established plan provided through a multiple-employer trust. (Several commercial ventures, working with tax attorneys, have set up such trusts and maintain and administer them.) The employer makes a tax-deductible contribution to the trust, and the plan actuary determines how much total benefit can be provided to the employees for the dollar amount contributed, given the combination of death benefits and severance benefits you, the owner, want to provide.

> Contributions can be deductible as ordinary and necessary business expenses on the company's federal income tax return.

The trust uses the contribution to buy life insurance for each employee, allocating premiums for coverage based on salary. The death benefits can be payable to the employees' families, and the value buildup can typically provide the cash for severance benefits, depending on policy performance.

A key feature of a welfare benefit plan is that contributions can be deductible as ordinary and necessary business expenses on the company's federal income tax return.

Assume, for instance, that Safe Seas Boat Works, Inc., a business with five employees, contributes $50,000 in the first year to a welfare benefit plan. Safe Seas can write off 100 percent of this contribution as well as additional contributions in subsequent years. What's more, these write-offs would be in addition to any gained from existing pension, profit-sharing, or SEP plans. Also note that the fewer the number of employees, the higher the percentage of benefits that can be allocated to the business owner. In the case of Safe Seas, where the owner is paid a salary of $200,000 and the employees are paid a total of $100,000, the owner would receive two-thirds of the benefits.

With welfare benefit plans, funding costs can often be reduced after a first-year lump-sum contribution sufficient to begin providing the life insurance and severance benefits. This first-year lump-sum contribution is not mandatory, but it could maximize the initial tax deduction and reduce the future cost of funding a company's plan. (As a word of caution, the IRS has indicated they are going to carefully review plans that provide first-year lump-sum contributions over and above the normal cost. A more conservative approach might be to pay the cost of the plan on an annual basis.)

After the initial contribution, additional annual contributions generally must be made to cover the cost of life insurance benefits. The cost of severance benefits could be covered by growth in the cash value of the insurance policies, and, at some point depending on policy performance, further contributions may not be needed. Thus, the company could manage its contributions easily, either increasing or decreasing them annually. This can be attractive, given the potential for business setbacks and cash flow crunches.

Here are some other costs and benefits associated with welfare benefit plans:

- The insurance company providing the policies offers guaranteed benefits, which can help reduce the employer's liability. For example, assume Jacobs Contracting offers employees 300 percent of salary as a death benefit. This amount can be made available through life insurance based on guaranteed rates and costs guaranteed by the insurance company.

- Death benefits are based on a salary multiple and, if conditions are met, made to the beneficiary free of income tax and, potentially, estate tax. These benefits can be used to fund buy/sell agreements or create liquidity for the policy owner's family.

- Severance benefits are limited to twice the employee's annual pay in the year prior to employment termination. Plan contributions allocated to severance pay are

not taxable to the employee until the benefits are
received; then ordinary income tax rates apply.

- The employer's cost for plan administration varies. It
can be evaluated against tax savings. A typical scenario
might include a setup fee of $1,000.

- For any one employer, the cost of a welfare benefit plan
might be minimized if a single advisory and management firm handles the administrative and actuarial
work. Savings may also be realized by using group
rather than individual insurance policies.

There are cautions to heed with welfare benefit plans. The
IRS has stated (in Revenue Procedure 95-34) that it feels
that most welfare benefit plans covering majority owner-
employees are not able to meet the statutory requirements that
permit a deductible contribution. However, in certain cases, the
courts have supported the taxpayer, depending on the specific
plan design. Employers interested in joining these trusts
should seek the opinion of a qualified tax attorney. As with
any type of employee benefit plan, future legislation, regulations rulings, and/or court cases could alter the way these plans
operate. Perhaps the safest environment for a welfare benefit
plan might be a C corporation with two or more owners. S corporations and partnerships can also participate, but not sole
proprietors.

Welfare benefit plans are a relatively new development.
However, life insurance professionals and others specializing in
service to small businesses should be able to refer you to a plan.
As you review what is offered, remember that for the successful
growing business, these little-known plans can offer tax-wise
benefits to employees and owners.

Golden Executive Bonus Arrangements

In general, golden executive bonus arrangements are designed
to retain and motivate key personnel. Here's how they can work:
The RST Company pays key manager Fisk a bonus, which is
used to pay the premiums on a permanent life insurance policy
issued on Fisk and owned by Fisk or his spouse. The policy helps
provide protection for the executive's family against loss of

income due to death while also allowing for the accumulation of tax-deferred cash value within the policy—cash value that can be used by Fisk in the future without paying income taxes if the policy is not a modified endowment contract. The bonus arrangement works like this: When the annual premium comes due, RST pays it in full. At the end of the year, Fisk receives a W-2 income tax form for the premium paid, and RST deducts the premium—as long as it is an ordinary and necessary business expense. The actual cost to Fisk is the tax on the bonus. The cost to RST is the after-tax cost of the bonus. The key point is that, for the cost of paying taxes on the premium, Fisk owns the entire value of the insurance policy.

Clearly, the arrangement gives Fisk an added reason to stay with the company. The longer he remains, the more contributions are made on his behalf and the greater the value of the insurance policy.

To gain additional leverage over Fisk's use of the executive bonus arrangement, RST can restrict Fisk's use of the policy for a period of time. For example, Fisk may be permitted to change the beneficiary at his choosing but would be required to gain RST's written consent before taking other actions such as accessing the cash value.

Alternatively, a protective clause in golden executive bonus arrangements can provide companies with a means of recovering their costs if key employees fail to perform for a minimum period of service. It works this way: Apart from the insurance contract, the company and the executive agree to an employment contract specifying that should the executive leave the company prior to the end of a prearranged restriction period, the employer has the right to recover a specified amount of money. Note that this is an unsecured arrangement.

For the employer, golden executive bonus plans can offer several key advantages:

- The company incurs no regular continuing administrative costs and does not book an accounting liability when the arrangement is implemented.
- The company can recover some of its costs should it lose the services of the executive through attrition.

Golden executive bonus arrangements also have distinct advantages from the executive's perspective:

- The benefit is established as a fixed incentive and thus is not subject to the whims of the employer.
- Typically, the insurance policy will be immune from the claims of an insured's creditors (depending on state law).

Although golden executive bonus plans are attractive and can be effective in recruiting and retaining key employees, there are caveats. As you explore these plans, keep two things in mind: (*a*) It is advisable to vest the executive at least two years prior to the normal retirement age of 65 to avoid potential ERISA implications. (*b*) These arrangements are subject to changing interpretation by the IRS and the U.S. Department of Labor.

Key Employees/Executive Protection

People are the most valuable asset in most businesses. The skills, knowledge, ability, leadership, and judgment of key people develop and maintain the profitability of a business. Insuring material assets against loss, destruction, or theft is standard business practice. But, when key people die, become sick, or are totally disabled, their value is lost to the employer forever—the result is often disastrous.

Death of a key person creates problems, including

- Cost of replacement.
- Loss of sales.
- Impairment of credit.
- Shrinkage in profits.
- Possible loss of control to outsiders.
- Insecurity of employees.

There are three ways to offset losses created by the death of a key person:

- Use profits to entirely absorb the loss in the year of loss. (But will the profits be sufficient in that year?)

TABLE 2–4

Probability of Death at Various Ages

Key Person's Age	Chance of Death by Age 65	Ages of Two Key People		Chance That One Will Die Prior to Age 65	Ages			Chances	Ages			Chances
30	23%	30	30	41%	30	30	30	55%	35	45	60	44%
31	23	30	35	41	30	30	35	55	35	50	50	48
32	23	30	40	40	30	30	40	54	35	50	55	46
33	23	30	45	39	30	30	45	53	35	50	60	43
34	23	30	50	37	30	30	50	52	35	55	55	44
35	23	30	55	35	30	30	55	50	35	55	60	40
36	23	30	60	31	30	30	60	47	35	60	60	37
37	22	35	35	40	30	35	35	54	40	40	40	52
38	22	35	40	40	30	35	40	54	40	40	45	51
39	22	35	45	39	30	35	45	53	40	40	50	50
40	22	35	50	37	30	35	50	52	40	40	55	48
41	22	35	55	34	30	35	55	50	40	40	60	45
42	21	35	60	30	30	35	60	46	40	45	45	50
43	21	40	40	39	30	40	40	53	40	45	50	49
44	21	40	45	38	30	40	45	52	40	45	55	47
45	20	40	50	36	30	40	50	51	40	45	60	44
46	20	40	55	33	30	40	55	49	40	50	50	48
47	20	40	60	29	30	40	60	46	40	50	55	46
48	19	45	45	37	30	45	45	52	40	50	60	42
49	19	45	50	35	30	45	50	50	40	55	55	43
50	18	45	55	32	30	45	55	48	40	55	60	40
51	18	45	60	28	30	45	60	45	40	60	60	36
52	17	50	50	33	30	50	50	49	45	45	45	50
53	16	50	55	30	30	50	55	47	45	45	50	48
54	16	50	60	26	30	50	60	43	45	45	55	46
55	15	55	55	28	30	55	55	45	45	45	60	43
56	14	55	60	23	30	55	60	41	45	50	50	47
57	13	60	60	18	30	60	60	37	45	50	55	45
58	12				35	35	35	54	45	50	60	41
59	11				35	35	40	53	45	55	55	42
60	9				35	35	45	53	45	55	60	39
					35	35	50	51	45	60	60	35
					35	35	55	49	50	50	50	45
					35	35	60	46	50	50	55	43
					35	40	40	53	50	50	60	36
					35	40	45	52	50	55	55	41
					35	40	50	51	50	55	55	37
					35	40	55	49	50	60	60	33
					35	40	60	45	55	55	55	38
					35	45	45	51	55	55	60	34
					35	45	50	50	55	60	60	30
					35	45	55	48	60	60	60	25

Source: 1980 *Commissioners' Standard Ordinary Mortality Table*

- Build a sinking fund over a period of years. (But, death may occur before it is funded, and business cycles may make adequate long-term funding unfeasible.)
- Acquire key person insurance, purchased at affordable annual premium outlays. (In most cases, this is a far wiser approach.)

Key employee life insurance can provide working capital in the event a valuable employee dies. It can be used to help offset the cost of replacing the employee, purchase stock owned by the employee, provide salary continuation to the family of the employee, and, possibly, help the employee's family pay estate taxes. Key employee insurance can partially solve the other problems we've listed by providing an influx of working capital to the company at the precise time it is needed. Table 2–4 is a probability chart that lists the chances of at least one person in a group dying prior to age 65.

Typical methods used to establish the value of a key employee to a business include:

1. Proportionate contribution of the employee to profit.
2. Replacement method (part of which takes into account a variety of hiring and inducement costs).
3. A multiple of salary times a number of years of service (e.g., five years).
4. An average of the preceding three methods.

Who, then, should be insured in your company? Anyone whose death would cost your company money, hurt production, or lose key accounts. In other words, a key employee! And don't forget yourself; you may well be the "keyest" employee of all.

Discriminatory Diagnostic Expense Plans

Here's another opportunity to offer a small but often overlooked income tax saving program for yourself and your employees. It focuses on reimbursement for medical diagnostic expenses, which generally include medical, dental, optical, and auditory services provided in the absence of specified symptoms or complaints. The following items should qualify:

- Dental checkups and cleaning, including x-rays.
- Routine eye tests.
- Pediatric, school, and camp physicals.
- Routine gynecological visits.
- Preventive general physicals, including diagnostic blood tests, heart monitoring tests, etc.
- Travel expenses in connection with any of the preceding items.

Typically, these types of medical expenses are *not* covered by commercial insurers. Without a plan, expenditures by the corporation for diagnostic expenses for key employees or owners would be taxable to the employees or owners as salary or possibly as dividends. However, with a written plan, corporate expenditure for these expenses would be deductible and would not be taxable to the employee. Also, it is possible to limit coverage to a small class of key employees. (Only C corporation owner-employees are eligible for these discriminatory plans; owner-employees of more than 2 percent of an S corporation, partners in a partnership, sole proprietors, and owners of limited liability companies (LLCs) cannot obtain this tax-free coverage.)

Instituting a medical diagnostic plan is simple: The corporation simply executes a resolution in the minutes. Either direct employer payments can be made, or employee payments can be reimbursed. The plan should contain a standard "statement of administrators' rules" to govern claims and disputes. A dollar limit should not be provided, and the plan can be terminated later, if desired, without penalty. Such a plan can also be implemented under the umbrella of a "cafeteria" plan. The advantage of this technique is that the cost of benefits is provided with pre-tax *employee* rather than *employer* dollars. However, use of the cafeteria plan approach requires observance of nondiscrimination and other tax law requirements.

Deferred Compensation

A nonqualified deferred compensation arrangement can be a Smart Assets strategy for you as a business owner or for you as a key employee. It is a way to reward key employees who may be crucial to building and/or maintaining the profitability of your business.

What is nonqualified deferred compensation? It is an agreement between an employee and employer in which the employer promises to pay a deferred benefit to the employee at some time in the future for services rendered currently by the employee. Deferred benefits are unsecured. This means that the employer's creditors can attach the funds set aside to pay the deferred benefits. Key employees should only agree to a deferred benefit program if they believe their employer will remain solvent.

Deferred benefits almost always include retirement income that can be in addition to, or in lieu of, a qualified pension, profit sharing or 401(k) plan. Disability and preretirement death benefits can also be included in the benefit package. The deferred compensation arrangement may provide for a voluntary reduction in salary by the employee or can be paid for solely by the employer. Like other retirement plans, the benefit provided can be a fixed amount, such as $5,000 per month, payable for a specific time, such as 120 months, starting at age 65. Or the deferred compensation can be arranged like a defined contribution plan. This provides the employee with an income for a given period of time, such as 120 months, starting at age 65, that is based on the future value of the employee's account.

In a defined contribution arrangement, the employer or employee (or both) set aside a sum of money each month or each year and invest it, but the actual benefit is unknown because it depends on the future growth of those contributions over time.

Why Employers Like Deferred Compensation In addition to attracting and retaining the services of key employees, a deferred compensation arrangement provides many benefits for an employer, such as:

- Benefits paid can be tax deductible to the employer.
- Employee participation is at the discretion of the employer.
- The employer may be able to recover some or all of its costs.

- The arrangement requires no government approval and only minimal filing.

Why Employees Like Deferred Compensation In addition to retirement benefits, a deferred compensation arrangement provides the following benefits to key employees:

- It can be structured to keep retirement benefits in pace with inflation.
- It can satisfy all or part of the key employee's need for personal life insurance and disability insurance.
- It can defer income tax on all benefits until they are actually or constructively received by the employee.

Cost Recovery and Life Insurance Another Smart Assets strategy for a business owner is to informally fund the deferred compensation obligation by purchasing life insurance on the life of the employee. Life insurance may even be able to provide the employer with total or partial cost recovery. Total cost recovery can be achieved when the employer owns enough life insurance at the employee's death to recover the costs of paying premiums, providing employee benefits, and the cost of money.

A simple example may be helpful to show how a deferred compensation arrangement may work with life insurance. Suppose Mr. Johnson is a 45-year-old key employee working for Alpha Corporation. Alpha and Johnson have entered into a nonqualified deferred compensation arrangement. The agreement states that Alpha will pay Johnson a retirement benefit of $100,000 a year for 10 years starting at age 65. If the corporation is in a 35 percent income tax bracket, the retirement benefit costs the company only $65,000 annually because the benefits are tax deductible to the employer when paid to the employee. The total after-tax cost of the benefits paid to Johnson is $650,000.

Let's further assume that Alpha Corporation owns a $1,000,000 life insurance policy on Johnson's life. The death proceeds could be sufficient to reimburse Alpha for all or some of the cost of the arrangement. In other words, cost recovery can be converted into this equation:

Death proceeds paid to employer

– Cost of premium

– After-tax cost of benefits

– Cost of use of money for premiums

Gain or net cost

Graphically, the deferred compensation arrangement can be illustrated as shown in Figure 2–4.

Comparison with Qualified Plans   A nonqualified deferred compensation arrangement is sometimes used as a substitute for a tax-qualified plan. The following chart summarizes some of the most important differences between the two:

	Nonqualified Plan	Qualified Plan
Discrimination	Yes	No
Asset of business	Yes	No
Annual administration	Minimal	Yes
Early retirement penalty	No	Yes
Tax-deferred growth potential	Yes	Yes

Additional Strategies to Consider

- Sometimes an employer may want to segregate assets used to pay retirement benefits to retiring employees by creating a separate employer-sponsored trust. The trust could name an independent trustee who would be responsible for holding employer contributions, investing them, and paying benefits to retired employees according to the agreement. As long as the trust property is subject to the claims of the employer's general creditors, contributions held by the trust should not be considered taxable income to the employee. Informally, these types of deferred compensation trusts are called "rabbi" trusts (the first known case was a synagogue that established a trust to hold the deferred compensation funds and pay retirement benefits to its rabbi).

FIGURE 2–4

Nonqualified Deferred Compensation

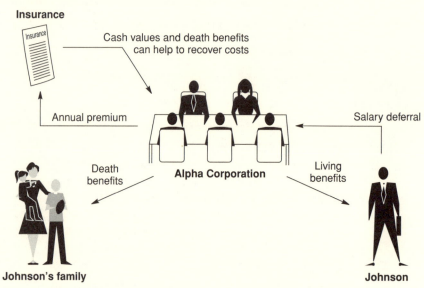

How a nonqualified deferred compensation plan works:

1. The corporation enters into a written agreement with a select group of highly compensated employees to provide certain benefits upon death and/or retirement.
2. The corporation is the purchaser, owner, and beneficiary of life insurance on each employee.
3. Contributions to the plan may consist of employer contributions, employee pre-tax deferral of salary, or a combination of both.
4. Life insurance proceeds are received by the corporation income tax free (except for the potential Alternative Minimum Tax applicable only to C corporations) and may be used to pay benefits in a lump sum or over a period of years.
5. Benefits, if reasonable compensation, are income tax deductible by the corporation at the time paid.
6. Policy values represent an asset on the corporation balance sheet and can be accessed by the business on a tax-favored basis if the policy is not classified as a modified endowment contract.

- If the employer trust becomes irrevocable and is beyond the reach of the employer's general creditors, contributions will be taxed to the employee as current income. These arrangements are called secular trusts and can be structured so that the executive's tax cost is paid by additional compensation. Due to this potential cost, secular trusts are not as popular as other arrangements.

- A deferred compensation arrangement for a corporation and a majority shareholder has been called into question by the IRS in Technical Advice Memorandum 8828004. The IRS stated that a controlling shareholder may be in constructive receipt of compensation set aside in a deferred compensation agreement. Furthermore, "a taxpayer who is a controlling shareholder is in a position to direct the corporation to do his bidding. He may at any time modify the terms of the deferred agreement, accelerate payments, or direct that any assets held by the corporation to provide funds to pay its obligations under the agreement be immediately distributed to the employee (himself). In reality, there is nothing standing between the taxpayer and the income. It is available at will." If you are a majority shareholder of a corporation, a Smart Assets strategy may be to avoid a nonqualified deferred compensation arrangement for you until this issue is clarified by the courts or the IRS. Despite the IRS's position, some advisors believe it is still possible to set up these arrangements by adding some protective measures, such as making the plan nonamendable except for a change of beneficiaries, requiring forfeitures of all benefits due to termination, and having an executive compensation committee represent the company when the arrangement is structured.

But now you may have a question: Does the deferral of income make sense if there is a possibility that tax brackets will be much higher at death or retirement, when the payouts are taxed? In many cases, the answer is yes. To see why, let's explore the case of Mr. Grant, the owner of a restaurant supply business.

Grant knows that he can comfortably contribute $10,000 per year to his company's program on a tax-deferred basis. He likes the idea of using pre-tax dollars for his retirement. His only objection is that he believes tax brackets will be higher, possibly much higher, when he retires. But his concern is ill-founded.

The truth is he could receive more retirement income from the deferral arrangement than if he took the $10,000, paid taxes on it, and saved the difference (depending on future tax rates) on his own.

There are two ways to illustrate that deferring income is the better approach. Assuming taxes increase prior to retirement, the break-even years method shows how many years income must be deferred for the deferral income to exceed the personal savings plan income. Assuming taxes increase at retirement, the future tax bracket method shows how high tax brackets can go while Grant still receives more income from the deferral plan.

> **Does the deferral of income make sense if there is a possibility that tax rates will be much higher at death or retirement?**

Break-Even Years Method Three factors will determine whether the deferral plan or the personal savings plan will be better for Grant:

1. The length of the deferral period (Grant is planning to retire in 20 years, at age 60).
2. The interest rate expected on the deferred funds (a rate of 7 percent is assumed for the deferral plan, and Grant is confident he could earn the same amount on his own in a currently taxable vehicle).
3. The estimated tax bracket when funds are distributed (Grant thinks future tax brackets might be as high as 45 percent in 20 years).

At Grant's current tax bracket of 35 percent with an assumed interest rate of 7 percent and expected tax bracket of 40 percent, providing he defers money for more than 5.5 years, the deferral plan will provide more income than the personal savings plan.

Future Tax Bracket Method The second way Grant can arrive at his decision is to do a simple calculation to determine how high the future tax bracket can go and still allow him to get more retirement income from the deferral plan. Assuming a 7 percent return on the company's pension plan (deferral and the personal savings option), the value of the deferral plan would be $438,652 in 20 years, and the value of the personal savings plan would be $234,923. As long as his tax bracket at retirement is less than 46.44 percent, it will make sense for Grant to defer his salary.

Here's the key point: the longer the investment period or the higher the rate of return, the higher the future tax bracket must be before the personal savings plan provides more income than the deferral plan.

Sole proprietors, partners in a partnership, and owners of S corporations would not benefit from this type of nonqualified deferral plan. They should use personally owned policies as retirement funders, with premiums paid from business bonuses.

Are you currently using smart plans to help motivate employees, reduce taxes, and build personal wealth? Now you know you probably should be; more than that, you have an overview of a menu of plans you can put in place in your business.

Why not sit down with your professional advisors now and put the appropriate plans in place. The sooner you act, the sooner you will be in position to accrue the benefits.

SUMMARY

Properly utilized profit-sharing plans, 401(k) plans, and other employee benefit programs can accumulate personal wealth for business owners. Age-based profit-sharing plans favor older and highly compensated employees who, typically, are the business owners. A 401(k) plan permits a highly compensated employee to contribute a greater percentage of salary than that of a nonhighly compensated individual. Nonqualified deferred compensations arrangements and executive bonus programs can be established solely for the benefit of key employees, which may include the business owner and members of his or her family.

The truly smart strategy for a business owner is to be cognizant of all of these retirement benefit programs, select the best plan or arrangement, and fund it with appropriate financial products. Often, we have seen that life insurance can be an important funding vehicle for many of those plans.

3

CHAPTER

Investment Strategies

Key Concepts Revealed in This Chapter

The Four-Step Approach
Building the Ideal Portfolio
Dollar Cost Averaging
The Search for Higher Yields—A Tax-Wise
  Alternative
Conclusion

THE FOUR-STEP APPROACH

Managed properly, your business can provide you with substantial income in the form of salary and profit, and if you sell your business, you may realize profit in the form of capital gains. But, important as this is, earning money is only one phase of building wealth. The other is to invest earnings in a manner that conforms to your needs and goals. To help you establish an appropriate investment strategy, we suggest the following four-step approach, which treats investing as a process.

Step One: Determine Your Objectives

Think about where you want to be financially in 5, 10, or 20 years and how much money it will take to support the lifestyle to which you are accustomed. The answers to these questions are critical because they can create financial targets.

Assume, for example, that you determine the need for an inflation-adjusted retirement income of $250,000. By calculating the asset values required to generate this amount of income by your target retirement date, you will know how much you will have to build your assets in the intervening years. This process applies to a wide range of financial goals, including:

1. Creating a cash reserve to protect you and your family for financial emergencies.
2. Setting aside money for your children's education.
3. Reducing income taxes on current investments.
4. Increasing your income flow from your investments.

Step Two: Analyze Your Current Financial Position

Analyze your current financial position, including the quality and categories of your assets and their exposure to risk. Then, factor in your income and tax obligations. This comprehensive view of your proposed finances helps to establish a financial baseline for future planning by indicating how far you have to go to achieve your goals.

Step Three: Create a Road Map

Once you know where you stand and where you want to go, you need a strategy and a series of action steps to achieve your objectives. Think of this as an investment road map. At the strategy level, your road map may call for such fundamental commitments as reducing living expenses to set aside more capital for the future, engaging in tax-saving techniques to help maximize income and investment opportunities, or recapitalizing your business. At the action level, these commitments should be flushed out with a series of proposed moves.

For example, consider the pledge to set aside a consistent amount of money on a regular basis. One approach is to engage in a pay-yourself-first program that makes monthly investments part of your bill-paying process. This way, saving becomes a necessity as opposed to a discretionary component of your financial affairs. Given the power of compounding, this could produce attractive results over time. Assume you invest $500 per month at a hypothetical 8 percent rate of return. With compounding, this investment could generate about $750,147 in 30 years.

Step Four: Monitor and Update

After embarking on your financial plan, review it annually or in the event of major financial changes, such changes could include significant business developments, a change in marital status, or new tax legislation. As you engage in this process, review objectives as well as results obtained to date. Assume, for example, that your financial strategy is geared toward accumulating $2,000,000 by age 65. Hypothetically, this could be based on a return of 10 percent annually. Midway through your goal, you discover that your portfolio is only averaging 8 percent. Potential solutions may be to change your investment mix to pursue higher returns or raise the amount of your monthly investment. Of course, any change seeking a potentially higher investment return usually means you must be willing to assume a greater market risk.

The knowledge you may need to adjust your course and what you will have to do to achieve your objectives, is the benefit you gain by carefully monitoring your program. You must bear in mind, however, that there are no guarantees, as investment principal and return will fluctuate with market conditions.

BUILDING THE IDEAL PORTFOLIO

To build the ideal portfolio for your personal needs, you should consider temperament, resources, and objectives. These steps should come into play:

1. Determine the degree of risk you want to assume.
2. Select the investment profile that best describes you.
3. Allocate your assets properly among different types of investments.

Risk and Reward

Given the wide range of investments available today, how do you select the ones that are right for you? Begin by comparing investments and weighing the potential risks against the potential rewards.

When you rank the major forms of asset accumulation vehicles, they form a pyramid. What is listed at the bottom of the pyramid should usually be the assets forming the foundation of your personal finances. This includes appropriate life and disability insurance protection for you and your family. As Figure 3–1 illustrates, as you move up the apex, investments are generally subject to fluctuation of principal, but they offer greater growth potential.

As you proceed, keep this in mind: A sound financial plan uses a variety of investments (in other words, "don't put all your eggs in one basket") and balances them in terms of risk and reward.

Investor Profile

Once you identify your personal investment profile, you will be in a better position to select the appropriate financial products. As you review these investor profiles, look for the one that comes closest to describing you.

FIGURE 3–1

Typical Investment Pyramid

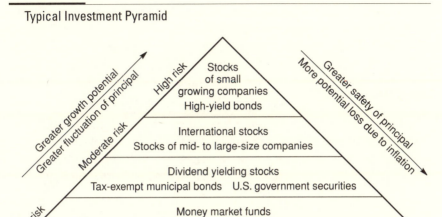

1. **Conservative.** A conservative investor generally has a short time frame and wants safety of principal. Typically, this includes retired people who depend on their assets for current living expenses and others who are uncomfortable with the ups and downs of the financial market.

   Types of investments: Money market funds, fixed-income investments such as U.S. government securities, and some stock holdings to help fight inflation.

2. **Conservative/Moderate.** This is someone who has a conservative temperament but can afford to be more flexible. This may be someone who has one or more children in college and has a significant debt to pay in a short period of time.

   Types of investments: Money market funds, fixed-income investments, and a slightly higher percentage of stock holdings.

3. **Moderate.** Moderate investors have a reasonable time frame to invest and can withstand some market volatility.

   Types of investments: A division between fixed-income and conservative equity investments. Conservative equity generally refers to larger, more stable companies (such as blue chip corporations), some of which seek to pay consistent dividends.

4. **Moderate/Aggressive.** This is an individual who is seeking a greater growth potential recognizing the higher degree of risk that goes with it.

   Types of investments: A majority of conservative equity investments, plus some fixed-income and aggressive equity investments. Aggressive equities generally refer to investing in smaller, more volatile companies that have greater growth potential and a higher risk potential.

5. **Aggressive.** The aggressive investor accepts a greater amount of risk for the potential of earning greater than average reward.

   Types of investments: A significant amount of assets allocated to aggressive equity investments, plus aggressive fixed-income and conservative equity investments. Aggressive fixed-income generally refers to lower rated, higher-yielding corporate bonds.

6. **Very Aggressive.** This is someone who can withstand the greatest amount of volatility while striving for the highest potential reward.

   Types of investments: A large percentage of assets allocated to aggressive equity investment, plus some aggressive fixed-income and conservative equity investments.

Bear in mind that investment profiles can change with your lifestyle and life cycle. For example, as you mature, you may become more conservative or more aggressive, depending on your personal situation. The key point is to know where you stand so that you can select the most appropriate mix of investments for your personal circumstances.

Asset Allocation

Asset allocation is a process designed to place your assets in the appropriate mix of investments.

It can sometimes be provided through mutual funds. Mutual funds pool your money with other investors to create a diversified portfolio of securities. Within a single mutual fund family, there may be many individual funds available for building your personal asset allocation. For example, a family may offer the following portfolios:

1. *Small company.* In general, this type of fund invests in common stocks of small companies that are undervalued in the marketplace. The companies may have a market capitalization of less than a specific sum, such as $1 billion, using a value-oriented approach.

2. *Capital appreciation.* This type of fund would normally invest in common stocks of growing mid-size companies that show accelerated earnings and other financial characteristics.

3. *International growth.* This type of fund invests primarily in diversified non–U.S. equity securities. They could be securities of companies located in Asia, Europe, or South America. Note: Political, economic, and currency risk is associated with international investing.

4. *Growth.* A growth fund invests primarily in common stock of mid- to large-size companies that demonstrate growth characteristics.

5. *Growth and income.* A growth and income fund invests primarily in stocks that pay dividends.

6. *Managed.* This type of fund invests primarily in a combination of stocks, bonds, and cash equivalents that are usually designed to achieve capital appreciation and current income.

7. *High-yield bond.* A high-yield bond portfolio invests primarily in lower-grade, higher-yielding corporate bonds.[1]

---

1. Higher level of risk including credit risk and price volatility associated with high-yield bond fund.

8. *Tax-exempt income.* A tax-exempt fund invests primarily in municipal bonds where the income is generally exempt from federal income tax.[2]

9. *Government securities.* A government securities fund invests primarily in securities of the U.S. government and its agencies to provide current income.

10. *Money market.* A money market fund invests primarily in short-term money market securities. Investments in money market funds are neither insured nor guaranteed by the U.S. government, and there is no assurance that they can maintain a stable net asset value.

How to Use Asset Allocation

These 10 typical types of funds can be mixed and matched in many ways to help achieve four basic investment objectives:

- *Aggressive growth.* You seek higher than average growth and accept higher than average risk.
- *Growth.* You seek to have your money grow over time.
- *Income.* You seek a steady current income.
- *Safety of principal.* You accept a lower rate of return for less volatility of your principal.

The "secret" to wise asset allocation is to adjust or allocate your portfolio to match your investment objectives. Figure 3–2 can serve as a helpful guideline for considering the allocation that is best for you.

DOLLAR COST AVERAGING

Every investor, from conservative to aggressive, wants to buy in at the low end of the market and sell off at the top—"buy low, sell high." But even professional investment managers realize

---

2. Income may be subject to the alternative minimum tax, state and local tax, and capital gains tax.

FIGURE 3–2

Asset Allocation

1 — Conservative

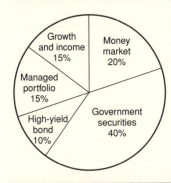

- **Key Objectives:** Safety of principal is very important. Often this type of investor may be retired. Also there is a need for steady current income as well as the need for some growth-oriented investments to help inflation.

- **Allocations:**

Money market:	20%
Government securities:	40%*
High-yield bond:	10%
Managed portfolio:	15%
Growth and income:	15%

2 — Conservative/Moderate

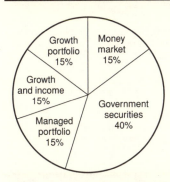

- **Key Objectives:** Safety of principal is very important. There is a need for a steady current income, but growth-oriented investments are also important to help fight against inflation and provide for later years.

- **Allocations:**

Money market:	15%
Government securities:	40%*
Managed portfolio:	15%
Growth and income:	15%
Growth portfolio:	15%

3 — Moderate

- **Key Objectives:** Steady current income is important as well as safety of principal. Often this type of investor has a growing family to support. Investing for the future is essential to help meet obligations such as children's college costs and retirement.

- **Allocations:**

Government securities:	30%*
Managed portfolio:	20%
Growth and income:	20%
Growth portfolio:	20%
International:	10%

*Investors in the upper income brackets may want to consider investing a portion of these assets in a tax-exempt income fund.

FIGURE 3–2

Asset Allocation (Concluded)

4 — Moderate/Aggressive

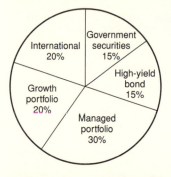

- **Key Objectives:** Steady, moderate growth over time is important. Usually this type of investor has a family and the children's future to think about.

- **Allocations:**

Government securities:	15%
High-yield bond:	15%
Managed portfolio:	30%
Growth portfolio:	20%
International:	20%

5 — Aggressive

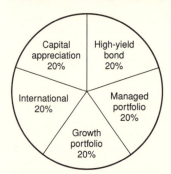

- **Key Objectives:** A higher degree of risk is assumed for the potential of greater than average growth over time. This type of investor is usually just starting out and has enough time to withstand the ups and downs of short-term market cycles.

- **Allocations:**

High-yield bond:	20%
Managed portfolio:	20%
Growth portfolio:	20%
International:	20%
Capital appreciation:	20%

6 — Very Aggressive

- **Key Objectives:** A higher degree of risk is assumed for the potential of greater than average growth. This individual is usually an experienced investor who has previously invested in the stock market and is comfortable with a greater than average degree of risk.

- **Allocations:**

High-yield bond:	15%
Managed portfolio:	20%
International:	25%
Capital appreciation:	25%
Small company:	15%

that it is difficult to consistently determine what is high and low. In fact, it is almost impossible to time the market.

With this in mind, most professionals take a long-term view, noting that "every time" is the right time to buy—if you buy regularly over an extended period of time. This technique is known as dollar cost averaging. The theory behind it is simple.

If you buy regular, fixed-dollar amounts—regardless of the current share price—you are predisposed to purchase more shares when the price is low. This means that, over time, you may be able to lower the average cost per share and take some of the guesswork out of deciding when is the right time to buy. This disciplined method of constant investing tends to curb the emotion to sell when the market declines. As Table 3–1 illustrates, with dollar cost averaging you are making the same regular dollar investments regardless of whether the share price is high or low. The effect of consistent investing is that you will typically purchase more shares when the price is low and fewer shares when the price is high.

Of course, no investment program can eliminate market risk, particularly during periods of market decline. Dollar cost averaging does not ensure profits in a rising market or protect you against losses in a declining market. But this method can help blend the highs and lows of market fluctuation and offer the potential for higher returns by lowering the average cost of the shares you buy.

Please note: Since dollar cost averaging involves continuous investment in securities regardless of fluctuating price levels of the securities involved, an investor should consider his or her ability to continue to purchase shares through periods of lower share price levels.

THE SEARCH FOR HIGHER YIELDS—A TAX-WISE ALTERNATIVE

One goal of Smart Assets is to potentially maximize the rate of return on your money. One way to do this is to utilize the way annuity products are taxed. For our purposes, let's briefly compare a single-premium deferred annuity (SPDA) and an immediate annuity.

A single-premium deferred annuity is a contract between

TABLE 3–1

Dollar Cost Averaging at Work

	Investment Amount	Share Cost (value)	Shares Purchased
Month 1	$500.00	$20.00	25 shares
Month 2	$500.00	$15.00	33.3 shares
Month 3	$500.00	$10.00	50 shares
Month 4	$500.00	$15.00	33.3 shares

Average cost for four months

$2,000 ÷ 141.6 shares = $14.12/share

Average price per share over four months

$60.00 ÷ 4 = $15.00

Total value after four months

$15.00 × 141.6 shares = $2,124.00

Four-month results: share value decline from month 1

$20.00 – $15.00 = $5.00 (25%)

you and an insurance company. In return for a one-time premium payment, the insurance company guarantees to provide you with a regular income at a future date. The interest earned on funds used to purchase a SPDA receives income tax deferred treatment. This means funds accumulating and compounding in the annuity are generally not taxed until these funds are removed from the annuity contract at the specified withdrawal age. At that time, your payment options may be a lump sum or monthly payments for extended periods of time. You are taxed on the gain in the policy when you take the money out. In addition, if you are under age 59½, a surrender may be subject to a 10 percent penalty tax in addition to income tax.

An immediate annuity is also a contract with an insurance company to pay out a specified sum on a monthly or yearly basis for a given period of time. Although there is no deferral feature, thus the term "immediate," these annuities are also taxed favorably. Each payment you receive is partially a return of principal, but you are only taxed on the interest element of the payment. Immediate annuities can be for almost any period of time. In the accompanying boxed example, we use an immediate annuity for a limited period of time, such as 10 years.

EXAMPLE

Let's assume you have a money market or certificate of deposit of $100,000 that earns 5 percent interest. Let's also assume you need $100,000 of permanent life insurance for individual or business reasons. After taxes your net income is $3,250 per year, (assuming a 35 percent income tax bracket). Instead of keeping the money market or certificate of deposit, you may want to consider the following Smart Assets strategy:

Take about one-half of your money in the CD (when it becomes due) or money market account and purchase a SPDA from an insurance company. Assume a hypothetical growth rate of 7.2 percent annually, which doubles your cash value in 10 years. Note: Actual interest rates vary and guaranteed rates (the minimum rate the insurance company will pay), if available, are usually lower than current rates. Unlike bank money market accounts or CDs, annuities have insurance-related charges and are not protected by the Federal Deposit Insurance Corporation.

With the balance of your money ($50,000), you purchase an immediate annuity with a short term payout of about 10 years. Let's further assume you can find another insurance company that would provide you with a payout of about $6,884 annually for 10 years. Each annuity payment you receive consists of a return of principal and interest. Income taxes are only paid on the amount of interest. Potentially, this could result in a net after-tax cash flow of about $6,224 for 10 years. This payout is hypothetical. Actual payout rates vary based on the interest rate in effect at the time the annuity is purchased.

After 10 years, the immediate annuity terminates, and no further payments are due. But, if your tax-deferred annuity doubled in value, you would have about $100,000 of cash value. If you still needed income, you could purchase another immediate annuity. However, if you surrender the tax-deferred annuity, you pay income tax on the gain, and, if you are under age 59½, you pay a 10 percent penalty tax on the gain.

As a result of this Smart Asset strategy, your cash flow could improve by about $2,974 annually after taxes. Here's where the life insurance option comes in. Suppose, for example, you are 45 years old and need $100,000 of whole life insurance. Let's further assume a life insurance company would issue this amount of coverage for about $2,052 per year. This leaves an additional $923 for you to spend.

Concluded

Based on this hypothetical example, you may have increased your yield and obtained needed cash value life insurance coverage, which may be critical to protecting your family. This table summarizes the technique:

The CD/Money Market Alternative

Option 1:

Certificate of deposit/money market	
Interest income on $100,000	$5,000.00
Income tax	−1,740.00
Net income	$3,250.00

Option 2:

Annuity alternative (10 years)	
Tax-deferred annuity	
Potential growth of cash value $100,000 in 10 years	$50,000 premium
Immediate annuity (10-year payout)	
Premium	$50,000
Potential annual cash flow (6.86% net annuity rate)	$ 6,884
Potential amount taxable	$ 1,884
Income tax	− 659
Annual after-tax cash flow	$ 6,225
CD after tax income	−3,250
Potential additional income over CD/money market	$ 2,975
Potential annual premium on 45-year-old male, nonsmoker, $100,000 face amount	−2,052
Additional money to spend	$ 923

This is an attractive way to leverage your existing assets and possibly accomplish some of your financial goals.

CONCLUSION

Accumulating assets through investing should be based on a Smart Assets process that includes establishing a plan and your investor profile, selecting the appropriate financial products based on that profile, diversifying through asset allocation, and utilizing dollar cost averaging.

4
CHAPTER

Tapping the Value of
Life Insurance

Key Concepts Revealed in This Chapter

Split-Dollar Techniques
Life Insurance Loans: Income Tax Advantages
Group Carve-Out
Primary Objectives of a Carve-Out Plan

As we have discovered, life insurance is an excellent way to protect the financial security of your heirs and can play an interesting role in pension and fringe benefit planning. But, that's just the beginning of the story. By exploring and implementing appropriate Smart Asset strategies, you will come to realize how life insurance can be used to achieve an even wider range of personal financial objectives, often building on our founding concept of integrating business and personal assets. With this in mind, you will want to view life insurance as a versatile financial tool that can be used in many tax-cutting and wealth-building strategies.

SPLIT-DOLLAR TECHNIQUES

Let's get down to specifics: Would you be interested in a technique that would enable you to benefit from the tax-deferred cash value built up in whole life coverage while you are alive and still maintain your policy's death benefit in full—and free of estate taxes?

As most people know, when an insured owns any part of a policy on his life, including its cash value, the death benefit is always included in the insured's estate and subject to estate tax. Nevertheless, you may be able to accomplish your goals through a technique known as *split dollar*, a frequently used and versatile method of paying for permanent life insurance that typically involves an employer and a key employee. The purpose is for the employer to help the employee obtain and pay for life insurance protection for the benefit of the insured's family while allowing the employer to reimburse itself for all premiums it paid. This arrangement provides for a sharing of policy rights, and a splitting of premiums and death benefits. There is an agreement to repay the employer's premium advance someday; thus, the employer may avoid any current charge to corporate earnings from an accounting standpoint.

> Life insurance is a versatile financial tool that can be used in many tax-cutting and wealth-building strategies.

FIGURE 4–1

Split-Dollar Arrangement

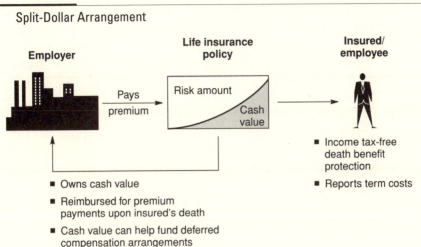

In most split-dollar life insurance arrangements, the employer pays the entire premium and owns all of the cash value. Upon the insured's death, the employer receives a part of the death benefit equal to the total of the premiums paid by the business. The insured's personal beneficiary receives the balance of the death benefit generally income tax-free. At retirement, the employer can surrender the policy and receive all of the cash value, give the cash value to the insured as compensation, or use the cash value to help pay a retirement benefit it may owe to the insured employee under a deferred compensation arrangement.

One important attractive benefit of the split dollar that makes it a smart business strategy for a business owner is that the insured employee obtains permanent life insurance protection and only has to report as income the cost of term insurance. The cost is measured by the lower of an arbitrary rate table, published by the government, called P.S. 58, or the insurance company's term rates for standard issue. In almost all situations, the insurance company's rates are lower than the P.S. 58 rate and should be used to measure the economic benefit for income tax purposes. Graphically, a split-dollar arrangement looks like that shown in Figure 4–1.

Split dollar can work extremely well for an owner-employee seeking to use low-taxed C corporation dollars while simultaneously minimizing the amount of personal taxable income. If the corporation is in a lower tax bracket than the owner, it makes financial sense to use or spend corporate dollars for a personal benefit.

Employer Advantages

- It aids retention of your firm's most valuable asset—key employees.
- Participant(s) can be hand picked.
- No IRS approval is needed.
- Funds can be provided to help meet obligations under a business continuation agreement.
- Money can be provided to help replace key employee(s).
- There is control over cash value.
- All premiums advanced can be reimbursed.
- It can help pay estate taxes and other debts to preserve family assets.

Employee Advantages

- The employer shows appreciation of the employee.
- An income tax-free life insurance death benefit is paid to help replace income for loved ones.
- It is a special perquisite at low or no cost.
- It can be kept confidential.
- It can help provide funds for college costs, retirement, business buyout or estate liquidity costs.

Options in Split-Dollar Plans

Corporate Split Dollar

In split-dollar arrangements, life insurance benefits (typically cash values and death benefits) are split up between two or more parties. Under a corporate split-dollar approach, the company—in this case your business—pays the premiums and owns the policy's cash value (see Table 4–1).

TABLE 4–1

Split the Premiums—Split the Policy

Employer	Employee
Pays most of premium (or all of it)	Pays term cost of coverage (or tax on term cost)
May bonus employee's tax cost	
Owns all cash value	Generally no cash value
Will be reimbursed for all costs, live or die (depending on policy performance)	Generally receives most of death benefi

Under ordinary circumstances, the insured, as owner of part of the policy, would possess an *incident of ownership*, meaning that all or part of the benefit would be included in his or her taxable estate. However, if the insured utilizes a Smart Assets strategy by having a third party (such as an irrevocable trust, custodial account, or adult child) serve as owner of the policy death benefit, he or she would not possess an incident of ownership and the policy would not be subject to estate taxes.

That, as we have said, is the case under ordinary circumstances. Your situation may be different—and more challenging. If the insured is a majority or sole shareholder of the corporation entering into the split-dollar arrangement with a trust or other third party, the company's ownership rights can be attributed to the insured through his or her stock ownership. This would cause the entire policy to be subject to estate taxes.

But here, too, creative strategies can overcome an apparent hurdle. For example, as the insured, you can reduce your ownership interest in the company to 50 percent or less by giving 50 percent or more of the stock to your spouse. Alternatively, this can be accomplished by gifting shares of stock to family members or selling shares to other co-shareholders.

A modified split-dollar arrangement can also be utilized. It works this way: If the corporation is not given the right to withdraw cash value, to borrow or pledge against it, or to surrender any portion of it, no incident of ownership should be attributed to a majority shareholder.

Here's where the benefit of the insurance can be utilized to further build your business and personal wealth. The cash value of the policy can be used in any reasonable way by the corporation. This may include helping the company fund a non-qualified deferred compensation program for the insured's benefit or as a source of cash for any legitimate business purpose. The bottom line is you have created a tax-deferred repository of wealth-building cash, although arrangements with a majority shareholder may be less flexible if you want to remove the death proceeds from your estate.

Let's explore another scenario. You are the company's majority shareholder and are unwilling to reduce your ownership rights. Under these circumstances, use of the cash value is restricted. But even here, there is opportunity to be tapped. It works like this: At any point in time, the company can terminate the split-dollar arrangement. Cash value is converted into cash, which is then funneled into the company and is thus indirectly controlled by you, as the insured majority shareholder.

Family Split Dollar

This type of arrangement also qualifies as a Smart Assets strategy, although there are caveats and limitations. This is a "have your cake and eat it too" strategy. Under this type of split-dollar arrangement your spouse can own the cash value of a policy on your life, and your children own the death benefit. In essence, your spouse is like the employer; upon your death, he or she gets the cash value and your children get the balance of the death proceeds. None of the policy proceeds should be taxed in your estate, and only the unspent cash value would be taxed in your spouse's estate. The annual gift to the children should be limited to the pure term costs of the insurance death benefit.

One limitation due to this arrangement is that the insured's spouse is the owner of the cash value but is under no obligation to use the money for your benefit or for the benefit of the family. In addition, in the event of a divorce, the spouse would have the right to retain the cash value. If your spouse predeceases you, the cash value should pass to a trust or other third-party owner such as your children. This way, you would not wind up with an incident of ownership in the policy; this prevents the policy from ever being taxed in your estate.

Family Partnership

The family limited partnership is an estate-planning device that can enable you to transfer ownership of income-producing property—including interest in closely held businesses—to children or other family members on a tax-advantaged basis. Specifically, partnership interests gifted to children may remain under the control of the parent as a general partner but may be excluded from taxation in the parent's estate.

The family limited partnership can also be used to shift unearned income from high earning, high tax bracket parents to lower tax bracket children. However, the benefits of this transfer will only be secure if the children are 14 years or older. For younger children, income shifted to them will be taxed at the parent's rate. Here is a common example of a family limited partnership: A father and mother own real estate and lease it to a corporation that is also owned by family members, thus providing the parents with an income source. To shift rental income to their children, the father and mother can create a family limited partnership and transfer the real estate to it, taking back 100 percent of the partnership interests. The partnership interests can consist of 1 percent general partnership interest and 99 percent limited partnership interest. As general partners, the parents can elect to distribute the rental income to the partners of the partnership as they see fit. The father and mother can gift the limited partnership interests to their children over time and allocate or distribute income to the children as limited partners.

Family partnerships make it easy to transfer fractional ownerships interests in property, such as real estate to children. Consequently, a parent could have a small ownership interest in the family partnership but control the partnership as the general partner. Most of the partnership equity would be owned by children and grandchildren—as limited partners.

A family partnership can be an extremely creative and beneficial way for a family to own life insurance on the lives of parents. For example, assume a business founder has a 1 percent ownership interest in a partnership. The partnership purchases a $1,000,000 life insurance policy on his life, owned by and payable to the partnership. Even if the founder is the general partner and exercises day-to-day control of the partnership, only 1 percent of the life insurance policy would be included as part of his estate. What's more, during his lifetime, he would have access to the cash value of the policy as the general partner but could use that cash value only for the benefit of the partnership—not for his own benefit. Also keep in mind that a family partnership can be disregarded by the IRS if the partnership does not engage in bona fide trade or business or investment activity.

Additional Estate-Tax-Wise Ownership of Life Insurance

Let's now review some important Smart Assets methods of owning life insurance.

The Roulette Theory

This theory is based on the ability of an individual who owns an insurance policy on his or her life to make a gift of it to another person and then live more than three years after the transfer. If the insured/owner dies within three years of the gift, the death benefit is included as part of his or her taxable estate; should the owner live longer, the death benefit is excluded from the estate.

The roulette theory can work well with survivorship life insurance, which is issued on two lives and pays a death benefit only after the surviving insured dies. Survivorship insurance is often used to protect the estate of a surviving spouse. Because most couples utilize the unlimited marital deduction, estate taxes are not due until the surviving spouse dies. However, to fully shield the insurance from estate taxes, individuals will often transfer their policies to custodianships for minor children, to adult children, or to irrevocable life insurance trusts. This can achieve estate tax protection, but at a price. Specifically, the insureds lose control of the cash value. This is of particular importance with survivorship policies, most of which can develop high cash values because they often remain in force for many years (until the second person dies). If the policy is owned by a third party, it prevents the insureds from utilizing the cash value in the policy for lifetime needs.

Which brings us to another Smart Assets strategy: A husband and wife can retain ownership of the policy and control the cash value. When the first spouse dies, the survivor can transfer the policy to a third party. To avoid estate taxes, he or she must live for at least three years after the transfer. This is a gamble that the insureds must be willing to take—hence, the name "roulette." If the insureds are of equal age or the surviving spouse is older, there may be a high chance that the three years rule will not be met. However, if the surviving spouse is younger and in good health, there is an excellent chance that he or she will live for another three years. The access-to-cash-values strategy will be effectively implemented.

The Supertrust

This method of ownership involves the creation of an irrevocable life insurance trust that contains a limited *power of appointment*, which is given to someone the insured-donor trusts, such as a spouse or adult child. Under the terms of the power, the holder (let's say it is the husband of a donor) can appoint trust property to anyone except himself, his creditors, his estate, and the creditors of his estate. This means that the holder of the power can appoint all or part of the trust corpus to the family—or back to the insured—at any time, although there is no obligation to do so.

Thus the Smart Assets strategy. As the life insurance policy owned by the trust matures, substantial cash value can be built up. The special power of appointment enables the insured-donor to indirectly benefit from the cash value of the policy based on his or her relationship with the holder of the special power of appointment. Can the money be used for business or personal purposes? Yes. But note: This approach may be considered aggressive.

The spouse of the donor of the trust should never be given a special power of appointment if he or she is one of the insureds in a survivorship policy. As one of the insureds, the spouse could be viewed as having an incident of ownership in the policy. This would cause the life insurance death benefits to be taxed in the spouse's estate.

LIFE INSURANCE LOANS: INCOME TAX ADVANTAGES

Most of us view life insurance as financial protection in the form of a cash benefit paid at death. But as we have demonstrated, insurance is also a source of capital that can be accessed in the form of loans or against tax-deferred, accumulated cash values. And the news gets even better the further you explore the possibilities: Borrowing from this source of capital can be a Smart Assets strategy, especially when you consider that interest payments associated with these loans can be tax deductible.

Here's a case in point. Assume you own a life insurance policy. If you borrow from the insurer to pay premiums, interest-paid deductions are not allowed. On the other hand, if you pledge your residence with a bank for an equity loan up to $100,000, interest paid to the bank can be deductible if at least four of the first seven life insurance premiums are paid from unborrowed money.

> Insurance is also a source of capital that can be accessed in the form of loans or against tax-deferred, accumulated cash values.

And the picture gets brighter still. If you own the policy and borrow to buy *investments* rather than to pay premiums, interest paid on the loan is deductible up to an amount equal to your total income from all your investments, assuming the investments are not liquidated to pay premiums. The policy premium must also be paid with unborrowed money. Better yet, this deduction is not limited to income generated by the investments purchased by the loan. Rather, it includes all investment income that you, as the policy-holder, report.

If you have yet to benefit from these Smart Assets opportunities, what can you do at this point? Let's make two assumptions: (a) Your policy loan was originally used to pay premiums, and (b) you have an investment portfolio. Based on this scenario, consider the following approach: Liquidate your investments to repay the policy loan, and then, if desired, reborrow on the policy to buy the investments back again. This way you can establish that the loan was actually used to buy investments, and the interest-paid deduction should be available up to your total net investment income. This is an aggressive technique that should be carefully reviewed with your tax advisor. Note: Investments sold at a loss must not be reacquired within 30 days if the loss is to offset gains or be deducted up to the $3,000 limit. Borrowing from a single-premium insurance contract to buy investments, however, will apparently not generate deductible interest.

As a business owner, you have special opportunities to obtain interest-paid tax deductions on policy loans. Consider the following guidelines and opportunities:

- If the policy was purchased prior to June 21, 1986, and is owned by a corporation (whether C or S), it would appear under current tax law that corporate interest paid on loans can be deductible without limit (up to corporate income).

- If the policy was purchased after June 20, 1986, the interest-paid deduction is limited to the interest on a loan of $50,000 per insured "key person" (not per policy) for a limited number of key persons. A "key person" is defined as a corporate officer or 20 percent owner. The number of individuals who may be treated as "key persons" cannot exceed the greater of 5 individuals or the lesser of 5 percent of the total officers and employees of the corporation or 20 individuals.

- Regardless when the policy is purchased, the Taxpayer Relief Act of 1997 imposes a new rule with respect to cash value life insurance owned by a business. Under the new law, no deduction is allowed for interest paid or accrued on any business debt allocable to unborrowed and untaxed surrender values of policy cash. Fortunately, cash values on single life policies covering 20 percent owners, employees, officers or directors of the business are exempt from this new provision. Also, the exception applies to joint life policies covering a 20 percent owner and his or her spouse. The exception, however, does not apply to joint life policies on two 20 percent owners (who are not husband and wife).

(In both cases, the four-out-of-seven rule would have to be satisfied if the loans are used to pay premiums, directly or indirectly.)

- If you already own a policy personally and have borrowed to pay premiums, consider transferring ownership to your corporation (or set up a split-dollar arrangement with the corporation) so that the company controls the cash and loan value. Under this arrangement, the corporation may qualify for the interest payment deductions. Note:

If the loan exceeds your basis in the policy (meaning the cumulative net premiums paid), the excess will be taxable income to you, the policy owner, upon transfer to the corporation. To avoid this potential tax, you may want to repay the loan so it is no greater than basis before transferring the policy. You can also sell the insurance policy to your corporation as long as you are an officer or shareholder at the time of transfer, but you will have to pay income tax on any gain realized over cost.

- If your business borrows from the policy for trade or business purposes other than to pay premiums, the four-out-of-seven rule may need to be met, depending on circumstances. For example, you could use the loan to finance unforeseen repairs or for the replacement of plant or equipment. The interest-paid deduction would still be limited to a $50,000 loan per insured if the policy were purchased after June 20, 1986, *and* if the loans are taken from the insurer. However, if the business borrowed from a bank and merely pledges the cash value rather than borrowing against it from the insurer *and* the loan was used for trade or business purposes other than paying premiums, the $50,000 limitation may be inapplicable even if the policy was purchased after June 20, 1986.

Note: Sole proprietors and partnerships owning insurance apparently can also obtain an interest-paid tax deduction on a similar basis if the loans are used for trade or business purposes (under the preceding rules). However, much like any other individual policy-owner, no deduction is available if the loan is used directly or indirectly to pay premiums.

Caveat: As you explore the possibility of policy loans with tax and insurance professionals, bear in mind that any borrowing results in a reduction of cash value and death benefits. Extensive borrowing can result in large interest payments on the loan, which can make it expensive for the policy-owner to keep the insurance in force. In addition, if the policy is surrendered or lapses, the policy-owner is treated as having received all prior loans in the year of surrender. If the total amount of loans and cash value received upon surrender exceeds cost (basis), the policy-owner has to report the gain as taxable income. This underlines the need to be prudent and disciplined in all of your financial transactions and to be receptive to advice from experts.

GROUP CARVE-OUT

Now that you have a wider view of the value of life insurance as a versatile business-planning, wealth-building tool, are you interested in additional creative ways to pay for this coverage? Of course you are. The good news is that one way of making that happen is to restructure your company's group life insurance coverage.

Let's start from the beginning: In business, life insurance is often a valued benefit, especially for the company's owner, and everyone would like *the company* to pay his or her insurance premiums. But this poses a problem. The cost of providing this coverage can become high over time. This is especially true in the case of highly paid executives, businesspeople like you, whose earnings require large amounts of coverage (i.e., over $50,000) and whose tax brackets require that they pay the highest marginal tax rates.

This is where a Smart Assets strategy known as the "group carve-out" comes into play. In its simplest form, a *group carve-out* is a method of finding premium dollars (currently being spent on existing group term insurance) to purchase permanent insurance for business owners. This coverage can be used to meet a wide range of your needs from estate planning to family income protection. The bottom line is that if you need insurance and are hard-pressed to find the premium dollars to pay for it, a carve-out arrangement may be your answer.

> A *group carve-out* is a method of finding premium dollars to purchase permanent insurance for business owners.

PRIMARY OBJECTIVES OF A CARVE-OUT PLAN

A carve-out may accomplish one or more of the following, depending on its structure:

1. Provide additional benefits to senior employees (including the principals) in the form of accumulated cash values and post-retirement coverage.
2. Reduce the employer's cost of providing the benefit.
3. Reduce the employee's taxable benefit.

The fact is, reallocating dollars from group term insurance to permanent insurance for your benefit (and perhaps for the benefit of your management team) can make good sense, in part because of the drawbacks inherent in group term coverage. For example, group term

- Provides limited benefits for you and your key executives. Benefits may be perhaps one or two times your pay, and the death benefit is typically paid only if you die prior to retirement.

- May not be cost effective for you or your key executives. Taxes are a major culprit here, making group life insurance coverage more costly than you think because federal tax law treats group term life, provided as a paid company fringe benefit, as taxable income for coverage in excess of $50,000. So what appears to be a tax-free benefit actually costs you money.

The following chart illustrates how much income you and your employees must report for each $1,000 of death benefit paid for in full by the company in excess of $50,000:

Age	Annual Reportable Income
25	$ 0.96
35	$ 1.32
45	$ 3.48
55	$ 9.00
64	$14.04

Here's a case in point: The reportable income for $200,000 of taxable group term insurance for 20 years ending at age 65 could be as much as $32,280. This means you and your executives would have to pay tax on this sum.

Consider these additional drawbacks of group term life:

- It has a small chance of paying a benefit.
- It usually stops or is severely reduced upon retirement or severance from the company.
- It provides no opportunity for the company to recover its costs.
- It is not portable.

What if you could address all these concerns by providing superior individual benefits at a lower cost. You can, and that's where the group carve-out plan comes into play:

1. It can be more cost effective over time than group term.
2. The employer can provide a benefit specific to actual need.
3. The employer can be selective in terms of who can participate and what benefits to provide.
4. The participants gain the advantages of permanent life insurance as compared with term policies: flexibility, tax-deferred cash value accumulation, access to cash values, and portability.
5. The employer has the opportunity to recover insurance costs.

Here is how the plan could work for a small business owner with $250,000 of group term coverage: Group coverage would be reduced to $50,000, and the remaining $200,000 could be provided by the group carve-out plan. The following is a hypothetical example: For a 40-year-old, preferred-rated, non-smoking executive holding a policy with a scheduled annual premium of $4,232 at a 6.2 percent interest rate (5.0 percent guaranteed), the numbers are as given in Table 4–2.*

As illustrated in Table 4–2, by implementing a group carve-out plan, you will be providing yourself and other principals or key employees with permanent insurance in the amount of

---

*Note: Actual premium and interest rate may vary—the reader should always ask his insurance representative to provide a complete ledger illustration.

TABLE 4–2

Carve-Out/Group Term Comparison

	Present Plan	Group Carve-Out
Group term coverage	$250,000	$ 50,000
Permanent coverage	0	200,000
Employer after-tax cost* (age 40–65)	37,521	36,270
Employee cost** (age 40–65)	9,610	22,320
Illustrated cash value at age 65 (based on current cost of insurance and interest rate)	0	81,002
Guaranteed cash value at age 65	0	56,504
Post-retirement death benefit	0	200,000

*Assumes term cost equal to 50 percent of NY Table Y rates and 35 percent corporate tax bracket.
**Assumes Table 1 rates and 40 percent employee tax bracket.

$200,000, which accumulates cash values and provides coverage after retirement. For example, Table 4–2 shows that the individual's net worth could increase by $58,682 (illustrated cash value less employee cost but, time value of money not considered).

As a kicker, this superior plan is provided to the company at a net after-tax savings of $1,251. In this example, the additional cost is incurred by the employee, but the company can choose to use its savings to partially reimburse yourself or other key employees through an additional bonus, thereby reducing personal costs.

To repeat, with group carve-out, your company reduces the amount of group term life insurance it provides everyone to $50,000, and for key employees (including the owner); it then makes up for this shortfall by providing for the purchase of permanent life insurance coverage for these individuals, using employer and/or employee funding (depending on your objectives) to pay the premiums.

Here are the primary ways to fund this approach to providing insurance coverage:

- *Through a bonus.* In this scenario, the employee (yourself included) is paid an annual bonus, which is a deductible expense for the company. The employee uses the bonus (plus personal funds, depending on the policy cost) to purchase a permanent individual life insurance policy. The initial premium is higher than for a group term policy, but over the long term, the permanent policy should cost less and provide more benefits.

With this approach, the employee must pay income taxes on the bonus used to purchase the policy but now owns permanent life insurance that can be expected to build cash value on a tax-deferred basis. This cash value generally can be withdrawn or borrowed on a tax-favored basis, and the death benefit is not subject to income tax. Estate tax inclusion of the death proceeds may be avoided by third party ownership.

- *Through an employer-owned policy*. In this arrangement, the employer pays the nondeductible premiums, owns the policy, and is the beneficiary; the employee need not report the premium payments as income. Death benefits paid to the company upon the death of the employee help the employer recover its premium costs and provide a deductible death benefit to the employee's beneficiary (who pays income tax on all amounts received from the employer). Should the company want to reward an employee (including the owner as an employee) at retirement, the policy's cash value can be used as a retirement benefit deductible by the employer if reasonable compensation and included as income to the employee.

  Usually, insurance death benefits paid to a C corporation are income-tax free, unless they attract an alternative minimum tax (AMT). Under the Taxpayer Relief Act of 1997, the AMT has been repealed for "small" corporations, generally defined as those having average gross revenues under $7.5 million after 1997. Generally, for corporations whose revenues exceed this amount, any AMT paid by them in a given year can be taken as a dollar-for-dollar tax credit against corporate tax due in future years, with an unlimited carry-forward.

- *Through split-dollar funding*. As we have seen before, this approach calls for the employer and the employee to fund a permanent policy. The split-dollar approach is open to several variations. In one, the employer purchases the policies and pays all the premiums. The employer owns the cash value that builds up in the policy (to help recover costs and/or pay retirement benefits), and the cash value may be considered an asset on its books. The employee owns the remaining net death benefit and must report income for the value of the fringe death benefit. This income, however, is often less than if the individual had group term insurance. The employer may own some of the remaining net death benefit to protect the company in cases where the company could suffer financial loss from the employee's death and/or to recover its premium share.

Compared with group term life insurance, the advantages of split-dollar funding include tax savings for the employee. The employee gets an income-tax-free death benefit at very little cost over the years because the employee has paid only for the tax based on the value of the death-benefit portion of the premium (a typically relatively small amount). And the employer recovers all of the nondeductible premiums it paid, or even more.

All three of these payment methods—bonus, employer-owned, and split-dollar—offer the advantages of permanent life insurance coverage that can be structured with a level annual cost and provide death benefits and/or cash value to the employee's beneficiaries and/or the employer. From the perspective of the business owner, key employee, or the company, group carve-out provides a surprise wealth-building and wealth-protecting benefit made possible through the savvy use of life insurance. This reinforces what we believe should be a key component of your financial planning: By exploring and implementing creative strategies—often by integrating business and personal assets—you can leverage the power of your resources and enhance your financial position over the years.

5

Shifting Assets

Keeping the Wealth in the Family

Key Concepts Revealed in This Chapter

Why Gift the Business during Life?
Estate Planning Enhanced by a Gift Program
Life Insurance Can Help Guarantee
  Planning Success
Estate Tax Rates and Credits
The Q-Tip Trust
The Irrevocable Life Insurance Trust
Gifting as Part of Estate Planning
GRITs, GRANTs, and GRUNTs
The Charitable Remainder Trust
Estate-Planning Summary
Installment Payment of Estate Taxes

Like most successful business owners, most of your wealth is embedded in your company. And as you know so well, a business must be continuously and competently managed. Which brings up to a key point: Sooner or later you will face the difficult question of whether and when and how to transfer the family business to the next generation—to either sell it to a family member, key employee, or outsider or simply to liquidate it. If you are inclined to keep the business in house, begin planning now. Acting expeditiously is important because there are many decisions to make and obstacles to overcome, including how to transfer the business during life without paying large amounts of gift tax or without paying a large estate tax if you wait until you die.

Let's tackle the tax issue up front. Combine the value of your business with your home, investments, retirement plans personal property, and other assets, and, if the total is over $600,000 (which is the exemption equivalent of your $192,800 federal unified credit against gift or estate taxes), you may have a tax problem! You or your estate will have to pay gift or estate tax on the business assets that you give or bequeath to others (most likely your children).

This may not be a penny ante matter. Considering that in 1997 marginal rates began at 37 percent, a heavy price tag will be paid for the privilege of giving the business to your children. But, as we have demonstrated, there are Smart Asset strategies for achieving many of your financial objectives—and this is no exception. Here's why: A new strategy for transferring family businesses, called *valuation discount planning,* can significantly reduce gift taxes paid during life and estate taxes paid at death.

WHY GIFT THE BUSINESS DURING LIFE?

Even if you want the next generation to have your business, the question asked is, "Why should I transfer the business during my life, if doing so means I will have to pay gift taxes?"

Actually, you may not have to. And even if you do, there are several reasons giving the business to your children is a smart idea. First, during life, you can control the transition process, including deciding which children should work in the business and how fast voting control should pass. To a large extent, you can also control how customers, suppliers, and creditors view the transition. Also, during life, the ability to minimize taxes by proper planning is enhanced.

Second, if you wait until death, your estate will pay an estate tax on the value of the business. Although gift and estate taxes are calculated from the same tax table, paying gift taxes on property transferred by you during life can be less expensive than accumulating the property and the gift tax savings in your estate and paying estate taxes on them at your death.

Assuming a world where there are no gift tax exclusions or credits and where there is only one tax bracket, 50 percent, the following example illustrates the cost of transferring a $2 million business to children during life and at death:

	Estate Taxes	Gift Taxes
Amount subject to transfer tax	$4,000,000	$2,000,000
Business value to children	$2,000,000	$2,000,000
Transfer tax due at 50% bracket	+2,000,000	+1,000,000
Total cost of transfer	$4,000,000	$3,000,000
Effective tax rate	50%	33.3%

The $2,000,000 estate tax is twice the amount of the $1,000,000 gift tax because, in a 50 percent marginal bracket, the amount subject to the estate tax is $4 million (business value + estate tax payment). This is why estates are called *tax inclusive*. The estate tax itself is included in the estate and is subject to tax. Gifts, on the other hand, are *tax exclusive*. This means gift tax is paid only on the amount of the gift and not on the gift tax, which comes from separate funds. As a result, the amount subject to gift tax in the previous example is $2 million, and the tax is $1 million.

Third, and often most important, giving a business to children during life means that all future business growth occurs out of your estate. Therefore, if the business in our example doubles, the growth is estate tax free. If this occurs, the tactic of shifting assets during life could save more than $2 million in future estate taxes.

Let's explore a hypothetical example: Mr. Granger owns a successful corporation worth $4 million and wants to keep the business in the family. To begin this process, he gives 20 percent of the business to each of his two children, gifting each child 20 percent of the company's capital stock.

Ordinarily, each 20 percent block of stock would be worth $800,000. But, because each block is a minority interest in a nonmarketable, non-publicly traded corporation, its value is less than what it would be as part of a 100 percent controlling block of stock, which would be much more marketable. Put simply, the sum of the parts of the business can be worth *less* than the whole. This is good because a valuation discount for gift-tax purposes can then come into play.

To obtain a valuation discount when gifting your business to family members, first have the business valued by a professional appraiser. Although the amount of the discount you can claim will vary depending on the facts and circumstances of each case, discounts for unmarketable, nonliquid, minority interests in family businesses can be as high as 40 percent (compared with what the stock would sell for if the business were sold or gifted as a 100 percent equity block). Table 5–1 illustrates how effective transfer tax rates can be reduced by using a valuation discount.

> The sum of the parts of the business can be worth *less* than the whole.

Further gift-tax savings can be achieved if your gift program is implemented over time. If a parent can give $10,000 annually, gift tax free, to a child, two parents with three children can give $60,000 per year free of tax. What's more, by using only a 25 percent valuation discount, they could transfer $80,000 of stock, valued at $60,000. Let's see how this factors in.

ESTATE PLANNING ENHANCED BY A GIFT PROGRAM

Consider the example of a 60-year-old business owner with a spouse, three children, and a $2 million family business that is growing at 4 percent per year. If, in the first year, the owner and his spouse transfer $80,000 of stock (4 percent of $2 million) to

TABLE 5–1

Reducing Taxes by Valuation Discount

	Gift Taxes	Gift Taxes after Applying a 40% Valuation Discount
Amount subject to gift tax	$1,600,000	$ 960,000
Business value transferred	$1,600,000	$1,600,000
Gift tax due at 50% bracket	+800,000	+480,000
Total cost of transfer	$2,400,000	$2,080,000
Effective transfer tax rate	50% ($800,000/$1,600,000)	30% ($480,000/$1,600,000)

their three children, the gift could be valued at $60,000, assuming a 25 percent valuation discount is applied to the gift. The $60,000 gift would be gift tax free under the $10,000 annual gift-tax exclusion because each child is receiving only $10,000 from each parent each year.

If the business continues to grow at a compounded rate of 4 percent per year, and if the gift program continues, the parents will be able to transfer 48.7 percent of the stock in the business to the children in 17 years. At the end of the 17th year, the business will be worth $3,895,801. The parents will own 51.3 percent, or $2,000,000, and the children will own 48.7 percent, or $1,895,801. The gift program effectively freezes the value of the business in the parent's taxable estate because the annual gift equals the 4% annual growth of the business each year. The parent's share of the business at the end of the 17th year would still be $2 million.

If the business grows for the additional one year, the corporation would be worth $4,051,633. At this point, further gifts might require the parents to give up majority control of the business to their children and create the potential for a "swing vote."

According to the IRS, a swing vote potential occurs in a gifting program when the minority stock given to two or more children can be combined to create a majority vote. In a 1994 private letter ruling, the IRS stated that the swing vote attributes of stock ownership must be taken into account in determining the fair market value of transferred stock for gift-tax purposes. In our example, this would have the effect of increasing the fair market value of future minority interests given to children. No swing vote potential existed in prior gifts because the business owner always had majority control.

Smart estate planning strategies can reduce, avoid, or defer federal estate taxes so that more of your property can pass intact to your intended beneficiaries.

Whatever value is placed on the 18th year gift, after the $80,000 gift, the parents would own 49.4 percent of the business, and the children would own the remaining 50.6 percent. At the parents' death, their estate (as a minority shareholder) would be entitled to a minority interest valuation discount on the value of the business included in their taxable estate.

For example, if the business was worth $4,051,633 after 18 years, the value of the parents' interest in the business would be only $2 million. At their death, however, the estate could be entitled to a minority interest discount in value. Using a 25 percent discount, the value of the stock in their estate would be reduced from $2,000,000 to $1,500,000 ($2,000,000 × 75). This value is less than 37.5 percent of the actual value of the business ($4,051,633)—thus, the powerful impact of the valuation discount Smart Assets strategy.

LIFE INSURANCE CAN HELP GUARANTEE PLANNING SUCCESS

Savvy business owners purchase life insurance to help ensure that their estate taxes are paid. If they don't, the family may have to sell or liquidate the business to pay the tax bill. In the previous example, the business owner's children might purchase $1 million of life insurance to pay estate taxes on the $2 million business value today. If the owner dies at any time before the 18th year and is in a 50 percent marginal estate-tax bracket, he or she would still be a majority shareholder, and the family would need the $1 million of income tax free estate protection (or more because actual tax rates can reach as high as 60 percent as values increase beyond $10,000,000) to pay estate taxes. Clearly, carefully planned asset shifting results in a wealth-protecting win/win for you and your family.

Why is this so important? Because without sound planning, the largest beneficiary of your estate may be the federal government—not your family. But it needn't be this way. Smart estate planning strategies can reduce, avoid, or defer federal estate taxes so that more of your property can pass intact to your intended beneficiaries.

ESTATE TAX RATES AND CREDITS

The federal estate tax is a progressive tax on the right of a person to transfer property at death. Fortunately, as we have noted, in 1997 every person is entitled to an effective $600,000 exemption from the federal estate tax. Put simply, the first $600,000 of property is not taxed. And, beginning in 1998, this exemption will progressively increase to $1,000,000 by the year 2006. Credit the Taxpayer Relief Act of 1997 for this. In 1997 through 2003, the next estate dollar in excess of the scheduled exempt amount will be taxed at a marginal bracket of 37 percent. In 2004 and 2005, the next dollar will be taxed at a marginal bracket of 39 percent and, in the year 2006 and thereafter, the next dollar will be taxe at a marginal bracket of 41 percent. The following charts summarize these rates.

TABLE 5–2

Marginal Estate Tax Rates Based on Actual Size of Bands of the Federal Estate Tax Table

Size of Taxable Estate				Marginal Rate (%)
Over	$ 0	but not over	$ 600,000	0
Over	600,000	but not over	750,000	37
Over	750,000	but not over	1,000,000	39
Over	1,000,000	but not over	1,250,000	41
Over	1,250,000	but not over	1,500,000	43
Over	1,500,000	but not over	2,000,000	45
Over	2,000,000	but not over	2,500,000	49
Over	2,500,000	but not over	3,000,000	53
Over	3,000,000			55

TABLE 5–3

Scheduled Increases in Exempt Amount and Unified Credit

Year	Exempt Amount	Tax Credit
1997	$ 600,000	$192,800
1998	625,000	$202,050
1999	650,000	$211,300
2000 & 2001	675,000	$220,550
2002 & 2003	700,000	$229,800
2004	850,000	$287,300
2005	950,000	$326,300
Thereafter	1,000,000	$345,800

In 1997, the first $600,000 of estate value is free of tax because the unified credit against the estate tax shelters the first $600,000 from taxation. This credit equals $192,800. Sometimes other credits may be available to further reduce the amount of tax due.

The federal estate tax is due nine months after death. Even with the scheduled increases in the unified credit, this may require your personal representative to sell or liquidate your property to raise cash to pay the tax. This is why planning ahead is so important. If you have to sell something quickly, or if the economic environment may not be suitable for selling, you may not realize a fair price.

The first step in developing an efficient estate plan is to know the value of your estate. Your estate includes the fair market value of your

- Home.
- Investments and other real estate.
- Life insurance.
- Business.
- Pension plan and other retirement programs.
- Tangible personal property.
- Property given away during life as taxable gifts.

TABLE 5–4

Marginal Estate Tax Rates Applied to the Next Estate Dollar
after the Exempt Amount

Year	Exempt Amount	Marginal Rate
1997	$ 600,000	37%
1998	625,000	37%
1999	650,000	37%
2000 & 2001	675,000	37%
2002 & 2003	700,000	39%
2004	850,000	39%
2005	950,000	39%
Thereafter	1,000,000	41%

Without knowing the size, extent, and value of your estate, it's difficult to develop an efficient plan. You need to know the value of your property to plan for potential estate taxes and to select the beneficiaries of your estate.

One important consideration for business owners is to know the value of the business for tax purposes. A business is often a closely held asset that is difficult to value. To help you determine value, a Smart Assets strategy is for you to retain the services of a valuation expert who can tell you how the IRS will value your company. Otherwise, the value of the business could be higher than what you thought and result in an unforeseen estate tax to pay after your death.

If you die without a will, your assets will be divided according to the laws of intestacy.

The next step to take in developing an efficient estate plan is to have an attorney draft an appropriate will and possibly a trust, even if it has to be changed or amended later. This step is critical: If you die without a will, your assets will be divided according to the laws of intestacy. Put simply, this means your state of residence at the time of death will determine how your assets will be distributed. Laws vary from state to state, but most jurisdictions provide that a surviving spouse will inherit only about one-third to one-half of the estate. The balance of the assets will go to your children, who will likely receive their share of the estate without restriction when they reach the age of majority (usually 18).

The problem with intestate distribution is that your assets are distributed according to a plan—but not a plan you have designed. For example, you may want all of your assets to go to your surviving spouse or most of your assets to go to one child as opposed to another. Here's the key point: Regardless of how you want your assets distributed, you should make that decision, not the state. And making a bad situation even worse, intestate distribution could cost your family time and money because of your failure to take advantage of the Smart Assets estate-planning strategies revealed in this chapter.

Understanding Will Drafting

A will is a legal declaration of intent specifying how you want to dispose of your property at death and whom you'd like to appoint as your fiduciaries. There is no time limit on the validity of a will. Once a will is legally drafted for a competent person, it remains valid regardless of where you live, when you die, or how long you live. Thus, if an 18-year-old person in New York drafts a valid will, lives for another 80 years, and dies in Florida, the will remains valid and governs the disposition of his or her property. Therefore, attorneys try to take into consideration the potential amount of time that may elapse and the events that may occur between the execution of a will and the time of its probate.

This time factor is addressed in any number of ways. If a parent wants to leave money or property to a minor, a trust is usually established under the will. The trust may postpone distribution of the property until the child becomes financially responsible. Prior to that time, the trustee of the trust may be given discretion to spend money for the child's benefit or make periodic distributions of income and principal to the child. Contingencies may also be provided for in the event the child marries, has children, and dies prior to receiving all of his property, or becomes disabled.

Even a simple bequest of money or property in a will can become complicated. For example, let's assume a parent wants to leave her daughter a diamond wedding band. A will may provide for different dispositions of the ring based on the occurrence of different contingencies.

For example, what if

- The daughter dies before the parent and has children surviving. Do the grandchildren share the ring? Does it pass instead to siblings?

- The daughter dies before the parent and has no children surviving. Does the ring pass to siblings equally or to another daughter?

- The diamond wedding band was sold by the parent. Does the daughter get the cash realized from the sale?

- The ring was exchanged for another item of jewelry. Does the daughter get the jewelry?

Ensuring what would happen in each situation takes time and skill when drafting a will or trust. Sometimes, the executor or personal representative named in the will is given the discretion to decide those issues.

Critical components of a will or trust for most clients of wealth include marital and nonmarital trusts. Generally, the intent of a testator (the person for whom the will is made) is to set aside the amount of assets sheltered by the unified credit against the estate tax in a nonmarital trust and have the balance of the estate pass to the spouse—or to a marital deduction trust for his or her benefit.

Two or more trusts may be needed to create the optimum marital deduction. In a nonmarital deduction trust, the will may describe the interests, if any, given to the surviving spouse and children with respect to distributions of income and principal. In addition, a trustee may be given discretionary authority to invade principal for the benefit of one or more beneficiaries based on their need. Contingencies such as the death or disability of a beneficiary should also be planned for in the trust.

The second trust that might be created under your will is a marital deduction trust. To qualify the property for a marital deduction, the trust must grant specific rights to the surviving spouse. Once again, the trust should carefully describe the interests of the spouse and those of the children who may inherit the property in the trust after the spouse's death.

Most wills grant executors and trustees broad discretionary powers with respect to investments of trust assets. This is done to give the beneficiaries an opportunity to benefit by authorizing the trustee to take advantage of what the trustee considers attractive investments. Since we don't know when a person will die or how long a trust may last, testators want their trustees to be able to buy and sell trust assets as financial markets and family needs change. Without specific authority in the trust, a trustee would be limited by state law as to what constitutes a permissible investment. Trustee powers are usually located at the end of the will.

The Need to Plan

Because estate-tax rates can be so high and are due so quickly after death, you may want ideas about how you can protect your property. Otherwise, your personal representative may be forced to write a check to the IRS for more than 50 percent of your net worth. Most people simply do not have that amount of cash available, or, if they do, their executors will wind up spending it on taxes instead of productive investments for their families. Reducing, avoiding, deferring, or having the tax paid efficiently may require implementation of one or more of the Smart Asset strategies discussed in the following sections.

THE Q-TIP TRUST

As previously discussed, one of the key aspects of estate planning is the unlimited marital deduction in which property that is transferred to a surviving spouse (who is a U.S. citizen) is not currently subject to an estate tax, regardless of the size of the estate. Many married people want to transfer their assets to their surviving spouse. However, from a tax-planning perspective, this may not be appropriate because the surviving spouse's estate may increase in value and be subject to a higher marginal rate of tax.

In some situations, such as a second marriage, one spouse may want to provide funds for the surviving second spouse but also ensure that the children of the first marriage inherit these funds after the second spouse's death. This can be accomplished through a technique called the "Q-tip" trust. To use this type of trust, the surviving spouse must be provided with all the income from trust assets for life. At the surviving spouse's death, the trust corpus (trust property) is distributed to the designated beneficiaries. The key points are (*a*) the spouse has no control over the ultimate distribution of trust assets but receives income for life, and (*b*) the trust qualifies for the unlimited marital deduction. This means the estate tax is deferred to the time of the surviving spouse's death and trust property eventually passes to the right family members.

For example, let's look at a hypothetical case study in which one spouse accumulates $1.2 million of assets, dies in 1997, and leaves everything to the surviving spouse. Because of the unlimited marital deduction, no estate tax is due at the first death. Let's assume further that the assets in the surviving spouse's estate do not grow, he or she lives off the income and then dies, and the estate is distributed equally among the children. The value of the surviving spouse's estate is the same as before, $1.2 million.

> By creating a bypass trust, up to $235,000 in estate taxes can be saved in 1997.

After taking into consideration the unified credit against the estate tax, the net tax due the federal government is $235,000. This is the sum the children will have to pay within nine months of the death of the surviving spouse.

Now let's see how a simple technique called a *bypass trust* can save estate taxes. Let's go back to our hypothetical case study in which one spouse has accumulated $1.2 million. At death, a bypass trust can be created that will be funded with the amount of money sheltered by the unified credit ($600,000); the balance of the estate will pass to the surviving spouse, also sheltered from estate tax thanks to the unlimited marital deduction. Therefore, the marital deduction and the unified credit together shelter this estate from estate taxation (see Figure 5–1).

FIGURE 5–1

Comparison of Trusts – 1997

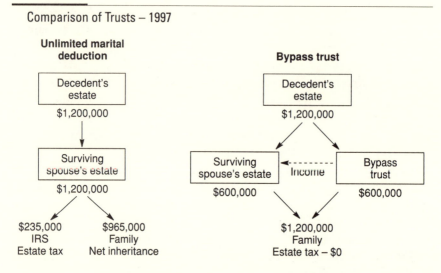

With this arrangement, a bypass trust has been created with $600,000 of assets. The trust could be designed so that all of its net income could be distributed to the surviving spouse for life, although this is not mandatory as it is with a Q-tip trust. In addition to income, the surviving spouse could be given a limited power of withdrawal, which is a right to invade the principal of the trust for the greater of $5,000 or 5 percent of the value of the trust. This annual right is forfeited if not exercised in any one year. Furthermore, the trustee can be given the discretionary power to use trust assets to provide additional money to the surviving spouse if he or she needs funds for health, education, maintenance, or support.

Clearly, the bypass trust can be designed to provide a surviving spouse with a range of financial benefits. The key to the arrangement, however, is that the assets in the bypass trust are not owned by the surviving spouse. Therefore, the value of the trust at this spouse's death bypasses the estate of the second to die and can be distributed to the children completely free of estate taxes. The only amount of property in the surviving spouse's estate is the sum received as a result of the marital deduction and, of course, her own property. In our example, this is equal to $600,000, which is the amount sheltered from estate taxes in

FIGURE 5–2

Comparison of Trusts – 2006

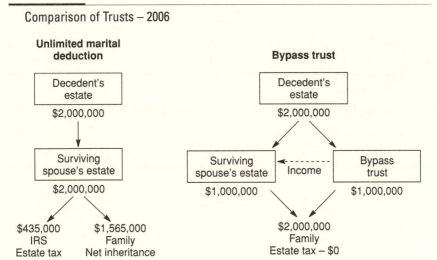

1997 because of the unified credit. Bottom line: by creating a bypass trust, up to $235,000 in estate taxes can be saved in 1997.

The increase in the unified credit will enable a husband and wife, who properly plan their estate, to shelter up to $2,000,000 (in 2006) from federal estate tax. This can be done by creating a bypass trust when the first spouse dies and funding it with up to $1,000,000 of assets. Compare this with a person who leaves his or her entire estate to a surviving spouse.

Another estate planning approach is to transfer your assets into a revocable living trust created during your lifetime. Generally, you are the trustee and control all of the trust assets. Because you control the trust, you are the owner of the trust property for income tax and estate tax purposes. The trust is not designed to save taxes. Instead, it saves time and money at your death because your assets do not have to go through probate before your family members can receive them. This can save legal and administrative expenses in settling your estate. It is also very important if you own real estate in more than one state. Without a trust, your executor may have to probate your will in every jurisdiction in which you own real estate. Also, at your death this trust can split into a marital and by-pass trust, as previously discussed.

FIGURE 5–3

Avoiding the Negative Estate-Tax Scenario

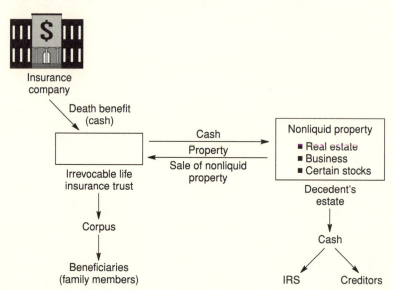

THE IRREVOCABLE LIFE INSURANCE TRUST

This planning device is the foundation for most estate plans because life insurance may be a large part of an estate. A life insurance trust is a separate legal entity that owns life insurance, usually on the life of the grantor. It is a popular estate-planning tool because, at your death, proceeds of the life insurance owned by the trust are used to protect your family and, if properly implemented, will not be part of your taxable estate or part of your surviving spouse's taxable estate.

Trust funds can be used to protect your family in several ways. Often, the primary purpose of the trust is to use the life insurance proceeds to help pay your estate taxes and other obligations your family may face.

As you have discovered by now, all of these strategies come with caveats and this one is no exception. Specifically, the trustee cannot be obligated to use trust funds to pay taxes, your debts, or the debts of your estate. This would cause the amount of money needed to pay these debts to be included in your estate for estate-

FIGURE 5–4

Providing Income to Surviving Family Members

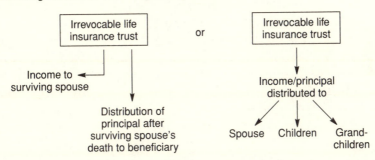

tax purposes. But just as there are caveats, there are also strategies you can use to mitigate their impact. For example, to avoid the negative estate-tax scenario, the trustee can purchase assets from the estate at fair market value (see Figure 5–3). After the sale, your executor has cash to pay the Internal Revenue Service and your creditors. The property sold to the irrevocable life insurance trust would either be retained by the trust or distributed to trust beneficiaries, presumably the same beneficiaries of your will. This way, your property can be retained by your family members because they are also the trust beneficiaries.

A second way the irrevocable life insurance trust is used for estate protection is to provide income to surviving family members. In this scenario, the trustee may be directed to reinvest life insurance proceeds and pay income to a surviving spouse or sprinkle income and principal among a class of trust beneficiaries consisting of surviving family members (see Figure 5–4). In the first option, the surviving spouse receives all income earned by the trust. Children or grandchildren, as remainder beneficiaries of the trust, would not receive distributions of principal until the surviving spouse dies. In the second option, the trustee is given discretionary authority to distribute income or principal to any member of a class of beneficiaries. The purpose is to allow the trustee to distribute money when and where it is needed. The drawback is that the trustee has control over the distribution of principal, and trust beneficiaries may or may not be treated equally.

Either trust design should be carefully considered when the document is drafted. This type of trust is *irrevocable,* meaning you, as the grantor, cannot alter, amend, revoke, or change your mind about it at a later time. Your attorney should review all your options and decide which is the best design for you and your family. Clearly, the irrevocable life insurance trust can be an effective estate-planning device. But beware of this: If you transfer a life insurance policy on your life and die within three years from the date of transfer, the death proceeds of the policy will be included as part of your estate. However, there is always *fine print* in this part of the law! For example, if the trustee is the applicant, owner, and beneficiary of the life insurance policy on your life, the three-year rule is not applicable. In the past, the IRS has argued that if the grantor is the source of premium dollars (through gifts made to the trust), which are used to pay for life insurance owned by the trustee, the three-year rule should be applicable even though there is no direct transfer of the policy by the insured. Several courts have ruled against the IRS, and this issue appears to be settled (the IRS stopped fighting). Thus, even though the insured/grantor may make gifts of premiums dollars to the trust that are used to pay for life insurance, the three-year rule is not applicable if there is no transfer of the policy.

We're not done yet. Life insurance owned by an irrevocable life insurance trust is also subject to estate taxes if the insured retains any incident of ownership in the policy. The regulations define an incident of ownership as

- The right to change the beneficiary.
- The right to surrender or cancel the policy.
- The right to assign the policy or revoke an assignment.
- The right to pledge the policy for a loan or the right to obtain a policy loan.
- A reversionary interest exceeding 5 percent of the policy's value immediately before death.

Thus, when a policy is transferred to an irrevocable life insurance trust, you as the grantor should assign all ownership rights to the trustee. Consider these additional points:

1. An incident of ownership can sometimes be imputed to an insured even if you do not personally own or possess any right in the policy. An estate-tax regulation specifies that if you are the insured and a majority shareholder of a corporation, any incident of ownership the corporation owns in a life insurance policy on your life will be attributed to you because of your stock ownership if the proceeds are paid to your personal beneficiary. (This is not the case if the proceeds are payable to or for the benefit of the corporation so as to be a factor in valuing the insured's stock in the corporation for purposes of determining the taxable gross estate.)

2. The insured/grantor of the irrevocable life insurance trust must also avoid having any control over the trust or receiving any benefit from the trust. For example, some of the following interests owned or retained by a grantor will cause the entire value of the trust to be included in your taxable estate (even if you do not possess an incident of ownership in the life insurance):

   - The right to receive income or trust property for life.
   - The possession of a probability of more than 5 percent that you will get the trust property back prior to your death.
   - The right to change or alter the terms of the trust or control a beneficiary's right to enjoy or receive the property.

   To avoid adverse estate taxation of trust assets, you, as the grantor of the trust, should not be a trustee, not retain direct or indirect control of the trust or trustee, nor have dealings with trust property. However, a recent IRS ruling (Rev. Rul. 95-58) allows the grantor to fire the trustee without adverse estate tax. This can give the grantor some control over the trust.

3. Gifts of premium dollars to an irrevocable life insurance trust are potentially subject to gift tax because they can be considered a future interest. To utilize the gift-tax annual exclusion, the recipient must have a "present

interest" in the gift, meaning he or she has the right to enjoy the property without restrictions. To create a present interest, estate planners give trust beneficiaries the right to withdraw a portion of the gift each year.

Each beneficiary can be given an annual right to withdraw up to $10,000 ($20,000 if the grantor's spouse agrees). The withdrawal right is usually limited so that it can only be exercised for a fixed period of time (such as 30 days). If the right is not exercised, it lapses. The trustee can then use the money received as a gift to pay the premiums on the policy. This concept, known as the Crummey trust, is based on the court case Crummey v. Commissioner. This technique makes a gift in trust a present interest gift as discussed below.

GIFTING AS PART OF ESTATE PLANNING

Once you've decided how to distribute your assets, planning ways to minimize your taxes should come next. Generally, it is difficult to entirely avoid federal estate taxes by giving property away during your lifetime. While there are benefits to giving, our tax system imposes the same rate of tax on the transfer of property during life or at death. But gaining an understanding of how our transfer tax system operates can help you plan your estate and take advantage of the few benefits afforded by Congress.

The Annual Exclusion

As we have noted, a major exception to the gift tax is the *annual exclusion*. Under this provision, annual gifts made to any one individual (valued at $10,000 or under) are not subject to tax. There is no limit to the number of people to whom $10,000 gifts can be made. If a parent has three children, he or she can give $30,000 each year without a tax. If the same donor is married and his spouse consents to the transfer, $60,000 can be given away by the donor each year. This spousal consent is called a *split gift*. If a split gift is used, the donor must file a gift-tax return (Form 709), and both spouses must sign.

To utilize the annual exclusion, the person receiving the gift must have the unrestricted control or enjoyment over the property. This is called a *present interest*. Conversely, if certain conditions are placed on a gift, the annual exclusion is not available. For example, let's say a parent gives $10,000 to his daughter but stipulates that she can't spend the money until she graduates from college. Since the donee does not have immediate access to the property, the gift is not subject to the annual exclusion.

The annual exclusion becomes a concern if you, as the donor, pay for life insurance owned by an irrevocable trust. If you pay the premium directly to the insurance company, it may be considered a gift of a future interest. Although the premium payment supports the policy in the trust, the trust beneficiaries would not have immediate control or enjoyment over the gift. To avoid a tentative gift tax, planners recommend the use of a Crummey provision in the trust (see page 98). In this case, you as the donor make a gift to the trust equal to the annual premium. The trust bene-

> It is generally difficult to entirely avoid federal estate taxes by giving property away during your lifetime.

ficiaries are given the right to withdraw the gift during a fixed period of time, such as 30 days. When the time period lapses, the trustee can use the funds in the trust to pay the premium (assuming the beneficiaries never exercised their right of withdrawal). The right of withdrawal creates a present interest in the gift by the donor to the trust and qualifies the gift as tax free under the gift-tax annual exclusion.

Using the annual exclusion is an extremely effective way to avoid gift taxes. Depending on the number of beneficiaries and the number of years you have to live, substantial assets can be transferred to children and grandchildren tax free. Unfortunately, there is often not enough time to reduce the value of a large estate through the use of the gift-tax annual exclusion. Most people do not plan their estates until age 60 or later. With limited life expectancy, a sufficient amount of gifts cannot be made to avoid transfer taxes on large estates. In addition, because couples may divorce or because one spouse dies, the maximum gift is often limited to $10,000 per year, per person, instead of $20,000.

Unified Credit

Gifts in excess of the gift-tax annual exclusion are called adjusted taxable gifts. They are taxable subject to a unified credit against the gift tax which in 1997 was $192,800. This means that in 1997 a donor could give $600,000 away during his or her lifetime and not pay a gift tax. The tentative tax on $600,000 is $192,800. The credit reduces the gift-tax liability to zero. The $192,800 credit is often called a $600,000 exemption equivalent. The Taxpayer Relief Act of 1997 has increased the unified credit from $192,800 in 1997 to $345,800 in 2006. The exemption equivalent will likewise increase from $600,000 in 1997 to $1,000,000 in 2006. Table 5–3 shows the scheduled increases.

Cumulative Gifts

The gift tax is structured so that donors are indirectly "penalized" for making successive gifts. The tax rate is progressive so that the larger the gifts, the higher the tax. Prior adjusted taxable gifts are added to the present adjusted taxable gift to determine a tentative tax. This requirement increases the effective rate of tax to pay on new gifts.

For example, a donor makes a taxable gift of $400,000 in 1997 after having made a taxable $600,000 gift three years ago. The tax on the present gift is calculated as follows:

Present gift	$ 400,000
Prior taxable gift	+ 600,000
Total lifetime gift	$1,000,000
Tentative tax on total gifts	$ 345,800
Less: unified credit	− 192,800
Tax due on present gift	$ 153,000

Since you, as the donor, are liable for the payment of the gift tax, it costs you $153,000 to make the $400,000 gift.

Gift Taxes and the Estate Tax

Similarly, if a person makes a taxable gift, the value of the gift at the time of transfer is added back into the taxable estate to "gross up" the amount of tax to pay. To illustrate how this works, let's assume a business owner made a gift of $1 million to his child 10 years ago. He filed a gift-tax return and paid $153,000 in gift taxes. He dies in 1997, leaving a taxable estate of $1.5 million. The federal estate tax is calculated as follows:

Taxable estate	$1,500,000
Adjusted taxable gifts	+ 1,000,000
Total taxable estate	$2,500,000
Tentative tax	$1,025,800
Less: unified credit	− 192,800
Less: gift taxes paid	− 153,000
Federal estate tax	$ 680,000
(State death tax credit not considered)	

The effect of the law is to treat the gift as though it were never made. However, there can be a tax benefit in making taxable gifts even if estate taxes have to be paid on them in the future. Suppose the property given away 10 years ago is now worth $2 million. Had the deceased entrepreneur kept the property, his estate would have increased by that amount and paid a higher rate of tax. Instead, by giving it away, he was able to transfer the appreciation out of his estate without tax. Thus, transfer taxes are saved on $1 million—the difference between the value of the property at his death and the value at the time of the gift.

The Gift-Tax Marital Deduction

Property given to a spouse (who is a U.S. citizen) during life is not subject to a gift tax. The amount is unlimited, so one person can give his entire estate to his spouse without paying a gift tax. For estate planning, the gift-tax unlimited marital deduction can be used to balance estate assets between a husband and a wife. In 1997, if each spouse has at least $600,000 of property in his or her own name, effective use of the unified credit against the estate tax can be maximized. Each spouse could then pass $600,000 of assets to children without transfer taxes. Therefore, with proper planning, you and your spouse could give up to $1.2 million to your children in 1997 without paying gift or estate taxes. This will increase as the unified credit increases. If a recipient spouse is not a U.S. citizen, the gift-tax unlimited marital deduction is, in effect, limited to $100,000 per year. However, the gift must be a present-interest gift for it to be gift tax free.

> Property given to a spouse during life is not subject to a gift tax.

Tuition and Medical Care Exclusion

In addition to the annual gift-tax exclusion, expenses paid by you for tuition or for certain medical care incurred by the recipient of your gift are not subject to gift taxes. The educational exemption is limited to direct tuition costs and does not include expenses for books, room and board, and other similar fees. The exclusion for medical care is only allowed for expenses not reimbursed by the donee's insurance. In both cases, in order for the gift to qualify, payments must be made directly to the applicable institution and not to the person for whose benefit the gift is made.

Planning Considerations

By using the annual exclusion and the $600,000 exemption equivalent, assets can be transferred out of an estate. However, transfer taxes should not be the only consideration; there are income tax considerations as well. A person who receives a gift succeeds to the donor's cost basis in the property. A beneficiary who receives a testamentary gift receives a step up in basis equal to the fair market value of the property at the date of death. This is an important difference. The cost basis of the property is extremely important in determining future income tax liability upon a sale. To make this easier to understand, let's look at a dollar and cents example.

Let's assume you give your child a building worth $600,000. Your basis in the building is $100,000. If your child sells the building for $600,000, he realizes a taxable gain of $500,000. If the child receives the property by testamentary transfer, his basis is stepped up to $600,000. A subsequent sale for $600,000 would result in no taxable gain.

Basis should be one factor to consider in deciding between making lifetime gifts and testamentary bequests. For example, if real estate values are unusually low, the time may be right to transfer assets that have depreciated in value. Lower values will save transfer costs if property will appreciate at a later time. On the other hand, if real estate values are high and are not expected to go higher, it may be a good income tax strategy to hold on to such assets for the step up in basis at death.

GRITs, GRANTs, AND GRUNTs

For many years, a frequently used technique to reduce gift- and estate-tax liabilities was the grantor retained income trust (GRIT). This device, however, went through various permutations, and the government repealed and then restored many of its key provisions, but for only certain types of property.

What Was versus What Is

Let's put this in perspective: The GRIT was an irrevocable trust that permitted you, as the grantor, to transfer property to it and retain all the income (or use of the trust property) for a fixed period of time, such as 5 or 10 years. When the trust terminated, the property in the trust automatically passed to a noncharitable beneficiary, such as a child or grandchild. The donee's (child's or grandchild's) interest is called a remainder and, for gift-tax purposes, a future interest. At the time the trust was funded, a "future gift" was made to the ultimate beneficiaries. To determine the value of this gift for tax purposes, the value of the "retained interest" was determined actuarially and subtracted from the full value of the property placed in the trust. Gift taxes were paid based only on that "remainder interest." Your interest is actually the present value of your income retained from the trust.

If you (the grantor) survived the term of the trust, the entire value of the trust was paid to the ultimate beneficiaries and removed from your estate. If you died during the term of the trust, the asset was included in your estate at its full date-of-death value. This technique was favored because it was seen as a "heads I win, tails I break even" situation. The property would have been in your estate anyway. But, if you lived, the property passed to the recipient as a gift valued at substantially less than the future value of the property.

For example, in a 5-year GRIT, the gift was valued at approximately two-thirds the actual value, while a 10-year GRIT resulted in a gift of approximately one-half; that's a win! Should you, the grantor, die during the determined term, the tax consequences would not be substantially different than had you never attempted to make the transfer in this fashion; that's a draw!

Congress recently effectively eliminated GRITs by stating that when an individual makes a transfer, the value of any "nonqualified" retained interest will generally be zero. Therefore (other than for "qualified" retained interests or the specific exception of a primary residence), the benefits of the traditional GRIT were eliminated. Under the new law, the entire value of the property would be considered gifted to the recipient for gift-tax purposes rather than the value of the remainder interest.

The new Tax Code provision goes on to say, however, that, in the case of certain qualified interests, the old valuation rules still apply. In these cases, the size of the gift for gift-tax purposes will be substantially less than the value of the property transferred. These qualified interests have come to be known as the GRANT (grantor retained annuity trust) and the GRUNT (grantor retained unitrust). Let's explore the differences.

In the GRANT, the grantor retains an "interest which consists of the right to receive fixed amounts payable not less frequently than annually." In simple terms, this means that the grantor can receive the same dollar amount from the trust every year, regardless of actual earnings and/or growth of trust assets. For example, 8 percent interest retained on a $1 million

GRANT would result in $80,000 paid to the grantor every year during the term of the trust or until the trust would have no money left. How much growth or income is actually earned by the trust is not relevant.

In the GRUNT, the grantor retains an "interest which consists of the right to receive amounts which are payable not less frequently than annually and are a fixed percentage of the fair market value of the property in the trust." In this type of trust, the payment to the grantor would fluctuate annually based on the value of the trust corpus. For example, if we set the valuation date for the gift at the beginning of the trust year and if the interest retained by the grantor is 8 percent, the grantor would receive $80,000 in the first year. The amount received in the second year, however, will depend on the value of the trust at the beginning of that year. If the trust earns $100,000 of income in the first year and only $80,000 is paid out to the grantor, the new calculation would be based on 8 percent of $1,020,000 or $81,600. Alternatively, should the income of the trust be only $60,000, the value of the trust at the beginning of the year would be $980,000, resulting in a payment to the grantor of $78,400, or 8 percent in the second year.

Just as with the traditional GRIT, the term of years selected is important when considering how large or small a gift is to be made. Let's look at a GRUNT where you, the grantor, are retaining a 6 percent interest. If the calculation is made based on a 10-year term, you are making a gift of about 56 percent or, in the case of a $1 million transfer, about $560,000. With a 20-year GRUNT, the gift is about 33 percent of the value of the property transferred. (Your tax advisor can accurately calculate the value of the gift.)

There is no limit to the number of years a GRANT or GRUNT should last. Here's why this is important: The longer the term of years, the smaller the gift being made and, therefore, the greater the gift-tax savings. That fact must be offset, however, with the increased risk of the grantor dying during the term of the trust, which would bring the assets back into the estate.

Insurance with GRANTs and GRUNTs

While the gifting leverage of GRANTs and GRUNTs allows them to stand on their own as effective estate-planning tools, their combined effect with an insurance program can substantially enhance an estate. Let's take a close-up look. There is always a possibility that you might die prior to the termination of your retained interest. The use of insurance to hedge against the inclusion of trust property in the estate is advisable. The insurance can be used to pay estate taxes or can be arranged to purchase the remainder interest from the beneficiaries.

THE CHARITABLE REMAINDER TRUST

A charitable remainder trust (CRT) is an irrevocable trust in which trust principal is used to provide benefits first to a noncharitable beneficiary and second to a charitable organization. Usually, the noncharitable beneficiary is the donor and his or her spouse. The interest they retain is either an annuity or unitrust interest, just like a GRANT or GRUNT. A minimum of 5 percent must be distributed to the donor each year. At the death of the surviving donor, the assets of the trust pass to the charity. A CRT is sometimes called a *split interest trust* because there are two different beneficiaries.

A CRT can provide substantial tax and financial benefits for a donor. First, the present value of the remainder interest payable to the charitable beneficiary CRT is deductible by the donor for income tax purposes. The remainder interest is defined as the right of the charitable beneficiary to receive trust principal after the donors' deaths. The amount of the deduction is complicated to compute because it can be based on the following factors:

- The fair-market value of the property contributed to the CRT.
- Age of donor and spouse (or other noncharitable beneficiary).
- Type of trust created.
- Amount of interest retained from the trust by the donor(s).

- Length of time the interest is retained.
- Applicable federal midterm interest rate in existence at the time the trust is created.
- Valuation factors published by the IRS.

A CRT can sell appreciated property without paying a capital gains tax. This allows the trustee to use all of the sale proceeds to produce income for the donor. More income can be earned by using a CRT than if appreciated property was sold outside of the trust.

Let's look at a hypothetical case study involving a husband and wife who are 65 years old. Let's assume they bought 1,000 shares of stock 20 years ago for $100,000. The stock has paid little in the way of dividends but has appreciated so that it is currently worth $1,000,000. The donors want to sell the stock and use the money for income, but they don't want to realize a capital gain on $900,000. If they sell the stock, they would have to pay $252,000 in tax ($900,000 × 0.28) leaving only $748,000 for investment. Assuming 7 percent could be earned on the money, this would produce an annual income of $52,360. Instead of selling the stock, the donors could contribute the appreciated stock to a CRT. The trustee could sell the stock, reinvest the proceeds, and pay the donors 7 percent for life. Since no capital gains tax is realized when the trustee sells the stock, $1,000,000 is available for investment. If the same 7 percent could be earned on the money, the donors would receive an income of $70,000 per year—$17,640 more than if they sell the shares outside a CRT.

> A charitable remainder trust can provide substantial tax and financial benefits for a donor.

In this example, the present value of the remainder interest given to charity is $261,400.* This amount is deductible from the donors' income. If the deduction could not be used in

---

*Assumes a 7 percent unitrust created when the applicable federal midterm rate is 6 percent.

the first year, it can be carried forward for five years. In a 39 percent tax bracket, the deduction saves $101,946 in taxes.

One major concern of a CRT is that a charity receives trust principal at the time of death of the donor(s). The donors' children are not beneficiaries. However, a donor could replace the value of the property given to charity by purchasing an amount of life insurance equal to the value of the trust. A donor could apply the tax savings and cash flow earned from the trust toward the payment of premiums. This way, the donors' family is protected and the charity receives needed funds. Figure 5–5 summarizes the CRT process.

ESTATE-PLANNING SUMMARY

Let's take stock of our estate-planning progress to this point:

1. You have learned that taxes can take a whopping hit on your estate (bad news).
2. You have also learned that planning can help to diminish the impact of the tax bit (good news).
3. You have discovered a series of Smart Assets strategies that can be utilized in the planing process (better news).

Now we must tackle another facet of the issue. Once again we are faced with a good news/bad news scenario.

Taking the bad news first, even with a well-designed estate plan, you may be faced with an estate-tax bill. The question is, "How will this tax be paid?" Three options come immediately to mind: borrow the money, dip into savings, or sell assets. These solutions, however, have built-in liabilities. Most important, all require that heirs pay the actual amount of the tax liability, or perhaps more. For example, if the tax bill is $1 million and if the heirs borrow funds to satisfy the obligation, they'll have to pay back the $1 million plus interest. In an even more depressing scenario, if they sell assets to pay the tax, they may have to consummate a sale quickly, accepting substantially less money than if they could wait for the ideal market opportunity.

But . . . and here's where the good news comes in . . . life insurance death proceeds can provide the cash so that the tax may be paid on an efficient basis. Taking this approach provides you with the following benefits:

FIGURE 5-5

Charitable Remainder Trust (CRT)

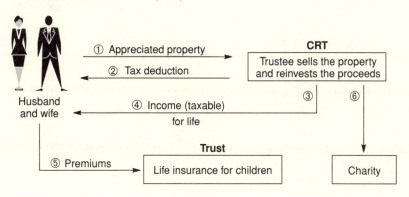

Steps

① Donor(s) contribute appreciated property to a CRT.

② The present value of the charity's remainder interest in the trust is deductible as a charitable gift from the donor's gross income.

③ The trustee may sell the appreciated property and reinvest the proceeds for income.

④ Trustee pays income to donors for their lifetime.

⑤ The donors can use the income and tax savings toward the payment of life insurance payable to their children or a trust for their benefit.

⑥ Charity receives trust corpus after donors' death.

- The certainty that funds will be available to pay your estate taxes (providing, of course, that sufficient insurance is purchased and that the policy is properly maintained.)

- The possibility that the death benefit may exceed the actual tax liability plus the premiums paid for the policy. For example, assume again that you are 55 years old and need less than $1 million of insurance for estate taxes. You purchase a life insurance policy with a $1 million death benefit. Even if you die at life expectancy after the policy is purchased, it's likely that your premiums will have totaled only a fraction of the $1 million death benefit that can be used to pay the tax. So the death benefit proceeds may exceed the sum of your tax liability plus premium paid.

In addition to a traditional single life policy, you can also purchase a survivorship or second-to-die policy. This policy is often ideal for married couples seeking to maximize their estate-planning opportunities. Similar to any other life insurance, both spouses apply for the insurance and both spouses generally must qualify (as to health) to obtain the coverage. The great appeal of this type of coverage for estate planning is that it pays upon the death of the second spouse—exactly when the estate tax is typically due. Because the policy insures two people, the premium is generally much less than the premium of insuring one person. It may also be possible to purchase second-to-die coverage with pre-tax dollars because, in certain cases, qualified plans (i.e., profit-sharing, 401(k), and possibly money-purchase or target benefit) can be amended to permit directed investment of these plans' funds into survivorship policies. Only the cost of the death benefit component of the coverage (in excess of the cash value) would be taxable income annually. However, at retirement or death of the first spouse, the policy should be sold or transferred out of the plan to avoid estate-tax inclusion of the death proceeds at the second death.

Clearly, insurance can be a critical component in your estate plan. Without the ready source of capital that the appropriate policy can provide, much of your assets may wind up with the tax collector. Premiums should instead be paid to purchase a policy with a death benefit equal to the anticipated estate-tax liability. Otherwise, your family may have to sell your business just to pay the taxes. To prevent these negative circumstances, consult with your tax, legal, and insurance professionals to create your own appropriate estate plan.

INSTALLMENT PAYMENT OF ESTATE TAXES

If you have a taxable estate and there is no life insurance or other liquid property for your personal representative to pay the estate-tax bill, it is possible that your estate can pay the amount of the tax attributed to a farm or closely held business over an installment period. The value of your farm or business must equal or exceed 35 percent of your adjusted gross estate. Interest on the estate tax can be deferred for up to 5 years, then the tax and interest must be paid over a period not to exceed 10 years. This installment payout is known as a Section 6166 election. It is based on Section 6166 of the Internal Revenue Code. If the farm or closely held business does not equal or exceed 35 percent of your adjusted gross estate, then the installment payment option is not available.

An apparent Smart Assets strategy is to try to qualify your estate so that Section 6166 can be used. However, you should be aware of the following:

- The tax deferral is only for the amount of tax attributed to the farm or business. The tax attributed to other assets is due within nine months of death.

- Even if the tax is deferred, it still must be paid with interest, which may affect the cash flow or profitability of the farm or business.

- If the installment payments are not paid in a timely fashion or if more than 50 percent of the business or farm is sold, then the remaining portion of the tax is accelerated.

- Until the tax and interest is paid, the IRS will place a lien on the business or farm.

- Estate administration expenses may be increased because the estate remains open until the tax is paid.

- The Section 6166 election should be avoided unless there is no other reasonable way for your executor or personal representative to pay the tax.

The Taxpayer Relief Act of 1997 has improved slightly the interest rate provisions of Section 6166 (see chapter 6, page 142). However, given the above concerns, it is still not the preferred method of paying estate taxes.

6

CHAPTER

Smart Strategies Under the Taxpayer Relief Act of 1997

Key Concepts Revealed in This Chapter

Capital Gains Tax Relief
Exclusion of Gain on the Sale of a Principal
  Residence
Tax Relief To Help Educate Your Family
Roth IRAs versus Deductible IRAs
Phased-In Increase in the Federal Unified Credit
Estate Exclusion for Family-Owned Businesses
  and Farms
Repeal of Pension Excise Taxes During Life and
  at Death
New 10 Percent Pass-Fail Test for Charitable
  Remainder Trusts
Interest Deduction Maintained for Business
  Loans Taken by Corporation That Own Cash
  Value Life Insurance
Improved Section 6166 Interest Rates
Miscellaneous Strategies for Individuals

After much negotiating and congressional debate, on August 5, 1997, President Clinton signed into law the Taxpayer Relief Act of 1997. A critical component of SMART financial and estate planning is to identify new tax laws and understand how they affect your business, personal finances and lifestyle. With this in mind, this chapter of SMART ASSETS is dedicated to providing you with special insight into the Taxpayer Relief Act of 1997 ("TRA '97" or the "new law") and helping you to identify new strategies that should be considered in light of this new legislation. In order to make this chapter as user friendly as possible, we have included strategies that highlight our best suggestions. Some of TRA '97's major reforms include:

- Lower capital gains tax rates.
- Increased tax savings on the sale of a principal residence.
- Significant IRA reform.
- New educational tax breaks.
- Estate tax reform for individuals and business owners.
- Pension excise tax relief.
- Charitable Remainder Trust reform.
- Many other provisions that could have a significant impact on your life.

To take maximum advantage of the important opportunities presented in this chapter and to avoid common implementation mistakes, we strongly recommend that you discuss these strategies with you financial advisors. Let's review the key provisions one at a time.

1. CAPITAL GAINS TAX RELIEF

Generally, long-term capital gains tax rates are reduced from 28 percent to 20 percent, and 10 percent for taxpayers in the 15 percent tax bracket. To qualify, assets must be held for over 18 months, instead of the traditional 12 months. Future capital gains tax rates can be even lower. Assets acquired after the year 2000 and held for more than five years will be subject to a

TABLE 6–1

Long-Term Capital Gains Tax Relief

Taxpayer Bracket*	Date Purchased	Holding Period	Maximum Tax Rate
Over 15%	Before 2001	Under 12 mo.	Ordinary Income
		12 mo. - 18 mo.	28%
		Over 18 mo.	20%
Over 15%	After 2000	Under 12 mo.	Ordinary Income
		12 mo. - 18 mo.	28%
		18 mo. - 5 years	20%
		Over 5 years	18%

*Including Taxable Gain
Effective: Sales after July 28, 1997

TABLE 6–2

Long-Term Capital Gains Tax Relief

Taxpayer Bracket*	Date Gain is Realized	Holding Period	Maximum Tax Rate
15%	Before 2001	Under 12 mo.	Ordinary Income
		12 mo. - 18 mo.	15%
		Over 18 mo.	10%
15%	After 2000	Under 12 mo.	Ordinary Income
		12 mo. - 18 mo.	15%
		18 mo. - 5 years	10%
		Over 5 years	8%

*Including Taxable Gain
Effective: Sales after July 28, 1997

top rate of only 18 percent and just 8 percent for taxpayers in a 15 percent tax bracket. Tables 6–1 and 6–2 explain the full extent of these changes.

Trap   Beware of special rules for special assets. For example, the 28 percent rate still applies to sales of collectibles held for more than one year, regardless of how long they are held after the first year. Also, gains attributed to depreciable real property will be taxed at a new 25 percent rate.

Strategy   Don't base long-term investment decisions solely on the current capital gains tax reform. Instead, make these selections on the basis of how they meet your overall financial goals. Over the past 20 years, capital gains tax rates have increased and decreased numerous times. Betting that rates will stay low until the precise time you are ready to sell is not sound planning.

For wealthy individuals, the new capital gains tax-rate structure creates a spread of almost 20 percentage points between the taxation of income assets (e.g., annuities, pensions, IRAs—a top rate of 39.6 percent) and the taxation of long-term capital assets (e.g., stocks, bonds, mutual funds—a top rate of 20 percent). A spread of this magnitude will undoubtedly result in an increased focus on converting ordinary income into long-term capital gain.

Trap   State income taxes on capital gains will generally increase as a percentage of total capital gains taxes paid. As a result, the "lower" rates may be more expensive that you think.

For those states that use federal adjusted gross income (AGI) as the basis of determining taxable income, state income taxes on long-term capital gains will remain at current levels but will increase as a percentage of total capital gains taxes paid. This favors wealthy taxpayers because they deduct more state income taxes in higher-income tax brackets than do middle-income taxpayers. Although states may decide to enact their own capital gains tax relief, many have not done so. Check the state income tax laws of your state.

Variable Annuities Remain Attractive

When it comes to saving for retirement, however, middle-income taxpayers should still favor variable annuities. For many taxpayers, the current rate differential between the taxation of income assets and long-term capital assets is only 8 percent (28 percent vs. 20 percent). Given the impossibility of predicting future income tax rates or of predicting the difference, if any, between future income tax rates and capital gains tax rates, tax-payers should still be better off selecting products on the basis of how well they meet overall financial goals.

Here's the key point   The benefits of owning a variable annuity are much more predictable than future tax rates and may well be worth *any* difference in tax rates.
  These benefits include:

1. The ability to fine tune or make major adjustments in your investment strategy without paying any current income tax.
2. The ability to lock in gains without paying any current income tax.
3. The ability to shift market risk to the insurance company at death.
4. The ability to create a guaranteed income that you cannot outlive.
5. The ability of certain holders of annuity contracts to protect their money from the claims of their creditors. (Depends on state law. Check with your local attorney for the rules in your state.)

2. EXCLUSION OF GAIN ON THE SALE OF A PRINCIPAL RESIDENCE

The exclusion from capital gains realized on the sale of a principal residence has been greatly expanded. Under the new law, a seller of any age who has owned and used a home as a principal residence for at least two of the five years preceding the sale can generally exclude $250,000 of gain (for a single taxpayer) or $500,000 (for spouses filing jointly). Table 6–3 indicates these changes.

  In addition to traditional residences, it would appear that the new exclusion can also apply to trailers, mobile homes, co-op apartments, condominiums, and boats with cooking, sleeping and sanitation facilities.

TABLE 6–3

Exclusion of Gain on the Sale of a Principal Residence

	Amount	Applicability	Limit
Prior Law:	$125,000	Taxpayers over age 55	Once in a lifetime
New Law:	$250,000	Single taxpayer	Every 2 years
	$500,000	Married filing jointly	

Since the equity in a residence often represents a major family asset, it is important to fully understand the impact of this new provision. While the new tax law may make it less "taxing" to sell a principal residence for taxpayers who have gains under the allowable exclusion, it may likewise make sales more traumatic for those with gains that exceed the allowable exclusion. That's because in the new tax law, Congress also eliminated the ability to roll over tax-free the capital gains income from the sale of an old residence to a new residence. Therefore, under the new law, if a single individual realizes a gain in excess of $250,000 on the sale of a principal residence, a significant capital gains tax might be due.

Strategy If you plan to sell your home to someone other than a family member and want to avoid paying capital gains taxes, plan to sell before you exceed the exclusion threshold.

Trap If you will exceed the exclusion threshold but plan to sell your residence to family members, selling part of your residence in one year and the rest after two years does not appear to keep you under the exclusion threshold. You should not be able to obtain two exclusions by selling your residence in two parts. The exclusion should not apply until the entire residence is sold.

Other strategies and traps may be quite fact specific. For example, suppose a couple has two residences—one in New York with a large long-term capital gain and another in Florida with a small gain. Suppose further that for the past five years the couple have qualified themselves as Florida residents—which is a common practice for income tax purposes. If the couple sold their New York residence first, they would not be able to exclude any of the gain from tax because for the past five years their principal residence has been in Florida. To avoid this result, the couple's principal residence must be moved back to New York and the sale delayed for two years.

Strategy   Consider making a gift of a non-principal residence to your children. Under the new law, parents can now give away that residence (which may require the use of some or all of their federal unified credit) to a child. The child and his or her spouse can avoid up to $500,000 of capital gain if they sell the residence after living there for at least two years.

Under prior law, one of the drawbacks of gifting a highly appreciated residence to children was that the recipient of the gift would not receive a step-up in cost basis when the gift was made. Instead, the donee would take on the donor's cost basis, which could be very low. As a result, a subsequent sale could trigger a sizable capital gain. The new tax law, however, gives individuals who want to "right size" their living arrangements and make gifts of their homes to children much greater flexibility to do so. If the child lives in the residence for at least two years after the gift and the gain is less than the excluded amount, the child should be able to sell the residence free of capital gains taxes. This result also can be accomplished through the use of a QPRT (Qualified Personal Residence Trust).

> Consider making a gift of a non-principal residence to your children.

Under the QPRT approach, parents can place their residence in an irrevocable trust and retain the right to live there for a specific period, such as 10, 15, or 20 years. When the trust terminates, the residence is distributed to the trust beneficiary, who usually is an adult child. Since the child will not receive the residence until a specific time in the future, the parents (as donors) will report a taxable gift equal only to the present value of the donee's remainder interest in the trust. This value is generally much less than the total fair market value of the residence. The actual value of the gift is determined through use of government tables and government-declared interest rates.

Strategy   If you give your residence to children through a QPRT, consider purchasing life insurance to help protect your estate against estate taxes.

Under this strategy, if you die before the trust ends, the entire value of the residence (gift value plus all future growth) will be included in your estate. Even if you survive the termination of the trust, estate tax will be due on the gift-tax value of the residence (but not the growth). In a real sense, life insurance can be the perfect hedge to QPRT planning. If you die too soon, the QPRT fails and estate taxes are due—but the insurance covers that loss.

3. TAX RELIEF TO HELP EDUCATE YOUR FAMILY

Four alternate forms of tax relief are now available to help families accumulate and pay for their children's higher education: The new HOPE Scholarship Tax Credit, the Lifetime Learning Tax Credit, the Income Exclusion for Withdrawals from Education IRAs, and the ability to deduct $1,000 of educational loan interest. In addition, beginning in 1998, withdrawals from traditional IRAs to help pay post-secondary tuition, fees, books, supplies, and room and board (for yourself, your spouse, your children or grandchildren) are free of penalty. The withdrawals, however, are included in taxable income. Each of these benefits is different. The challenge is to determine which are most advantageous for you and which ones you qualify for.

Strategy   Every year, enlist the advice of experts to help choose which educational tax breaks work best for you. Only in some circumstances are multiple credits available. Generally speaking, the tax break that's most advantageous for you will depend on your adjusted gross income and the amount and type of expenses you incur.

As indicated by the following summaries, the HOPE Scholarship Credit should initially be more advantageous than the Lifetime Learning Credit simply because it provides up to $1,500 in tax credits per qualified student versus up to $1,000 in total per year under the Lifetime Learning Credit. If you elect the HOPE Scholarship Credit for one student, you are precluded from claiming the Lifetime Learning Credit for that student in the same taxable year and precluded from taking tax-free distributions from an Education IRA for that student as well. However, using the HOPE Scholarship Credit for one student will not preclude you from using the Lifetime Learning Credit for other dependents, including yourself. Following are brief outlines of each benefit.

HOPE SCHOLARSHIP CREDIT

For What
Tuition and fees (not books, room or board, or transportation, etc.). For expenses paid after 1997, but only for the first two years of post-secondary education. Student must be enrolled at least on a half-time basis.

For Whom
Available for each enrolled student in the family, including the taxpayer, spouse or dependents.

Maximum Credit
100 percent of first $1,000 and 50 percent of next $1,000 (Maximum = $1,500 per student). Amounts are indexed for inflation after the year 2001.

Total Phase Out
$50,000 of AGI for single taxpayers
$100,000 of AGI for married taxpayers filing jointly
Indexed for inflation after the year 2001

LIFETIME LEARNING CREDIT

For What
Tuition and fees (not books, room or board, or transportation, etc.). Includes tuition and fees paid for courses to improve job skills. All expenses relating to undergraduate, graduate and professional-level courses must be paid after June 30, 1998. Available for an unlimited number of years.

LIFETIME LEARNING CREDIT continued

For Whom
Available for taxpayer, spouse and dependents.

Maximum Credit
20 percent of first $5,000 of expenses (Total = $1,000 until 2003)
20 percent of first $10,000 of expenses (Total = $2,000 in 2003)

Total Phase Out
$50,000 of AGI for single taxpayers
$100,000 of AGI for married taxpayers filing jointly
Indexed for inflation after the year 2001

EXCLUSION FROM INCOME OF AMOUNTS WITHDRAWN FROM EDUCATION IRAS

Contribution
Non-deductible $500 annual contribution on behalf of a designated beneficiary under age 18. Growth is tax-free.

For What
Tuition, fees, books, supplies and room and board for undergraduate or graduate courses.

For Whom
Designated beneficiary under age 18.

Distributions
Unlimited and tax-free to the extent it does not exceed the amount of qualified education expenses paid during the year the distribution is made. If a tax-free distribution is made in a given taxable year, a HOPE Credit or Lifetime Learning Credit cannot be claimed in the same year for the same beneficiary. Excess distributions are taxable and subject to a 10 percent penalty. The penalty is waived if the distribution is made on account of death or disability. Account must be fully distributed by the child's age 30 or rolled over to a sibling's account.

Total Phase Out
$110,000 of AGI for single taxpayers
$160,000 of AGI for married taxpayers

4. ROTH IRAS VERSUS DEDUCTIBLE IRAS

A Roth IRA is a new retirement savings vehicle that permits certain taxpayers to make $2,000 annual non-deductible contributions to an IRA that provides tax-deferred growth. In addition, under the Roth IRA, "qualified distributions" are paid *free of income tax*. A "qualified distribution" from a Roth IRA is made from the account after the fifth taxable year of the account *and* after age 59½, or upon the owner's death or disability, or to purchase a qualified first-time home ($10,000 lifetime limit).

> A Roth IRA can be set up for each spouse.

A Roth IRA can be set up for each spouse and, unlike deductible IRAs, can be funded even if the taxpayer is over age 70½. Also, subject to AGI limits, a person can establish a Roth IRA even though his or her spouse is a participant in a qualified plan.

Adjusted Gross Income (AGI) Phase-Out Limits—Roth IRAs

A single taxpayer can make annual contributions to a Roth IRA provided his or her adjusted gross income (AGI) does not exceed certain limits. The AGI phase-out limits for Roth IRAs begin at $150,000 for married taxpayers filing jointly and at $95,000 for single taxpayers. The ability to contribute to a Roth IRA is totally phased out for AGIs over $160,000 for married taxpayers filing jointly and over $110,000 for single taxpayers.

Adjusted Gross Income Phase-Out Limits—Deductible IRAs

The new law has also increased the AGI phase-out limits for deductible IRAs for taxpayers who are participants in a qualified plan. Effective January 1, 1998, for deductible IRAs, AGI phase-out begins at $25,000 for single taxpayers and is complete at $35,000. For married taxpayers filing jointly, AGI phase-out begins at $40,000 of adjusted gross income and is complete at $50,000. These limits increase progressively according to Table 6–4.

TABLE 6–4

AGI Phase-Out Limits for Deductible IRAs

Year	Individuals		Married Filing Jointly	
	Phase-Out Begins	Phase-Out Complete	Phase-Out Begins	Phase-Out Complete
1997	$25,000	$35,000	$40,000	$50,000
1998	30,000	40,000	50,000	60,000
1999	31,000	41,000	51,000	61,000
2000	32,000	42,000	52,000	62,000
2001	33,000	43,000	53,000	63,000
2002	34,000	44,000	54,000	64,000
2003	40,000	50,000	60,000	70,000
2004	45,000	55,000	65,000	75,000
2005	50,000	60,000	70,000	80,000
2006	50,000	60,000	75,000	85,000
2007	50,000	60,000	80,000	100,000

Effective: January 1, 1998

Additional Roth IRA Rules

- "Qualified Distributions" cannot be made until the taxpayer has had the Roth IRA in effect for at least five years.
- Non-qualified distributions made from earnings are subject to a 10 percent penalty tax before age 59½.
- If a $2,000 contribution has already been made to a deductible IRA, no contribution may be made to a Roth IRA in the same taxable year.
- If the owner of a deductible IRA has an adjusted gross income of under $100,000, he or she can convert the deductible IRA to a Roth IRA without penalty, and before the end of 1998, may spread the payment of income tax on the deductible IRA balance over four years.

Strategy If you qualify to make contributions to both a deductible IRA and a Roth IRA, consider funding the Roth IRA. All things being equal, a Roth IRA can provide more after-tax retirement income than a deductible IRA. This is especially the case if ordinary income tax rates increase.

Strategy If you are a participant of an employer-sponsored 401(k) plan and qualify to make contributions to a Roth IRA, consider contributing to the 401(k) first to the extent of the company match. Then contribute the next $2,000 to a Roth IRA and then, if possible, fund the rest of your 401(k).

Strategy If you do not qualify for a Roth IRA or would like to contribute more than $2,000 to a product that has a non-deductible contribution, tax-deferred growth and potentially no income tax on withdrawals, consider owning cash value life insurance. For corporate executives, consider a Section 162 bonus arrangement.

Table 6–5 is an example of how the performance of a Roth IRA can exceed the performance of a deductible IRA.

TABLE 6–5

Roth IRA versus Deductible IRA

Roth IRA

Contribution to Roth IRA	$2,000
Income Tax Savings	0
Income Tax Bracket	28%
Total Annual Investment	$2,000
Annual Investment Rate	8%
Years to Accumulate	20 years (age 45 through age 64)
Funds Available at Age 65	$98,946
Retirement Income Period	15 years (age 65 through age 79)
Annual Retirement Income	$10,692
After-Tax Income	$10,692 (no income tax due)
Total After-Tax Income	**$160,380**

Deductible IRA

Deductible IRA Contribution	$2,000 (beginning of the year)
Income Tax Savings	$560 (assuming a 28% tax bracket)
Total Annual Investment	$2,560
Annual Interest Rate	8%
Years To Accumulate	20 years (age 45 through age 64)
Funds Available at Age 65	$123,913 (includes $11,200 of tax savings)
Retirement Income Period	15 years (age 65 through age 79)
Annual Retirement Income	$13,404
After-Tax Income	$9,860 (assuming a 28% tax bracket)
Total After-Tax Income	**$147,900**

TABLE 6-5

(continued)

Contributions Deductible IRA

	Beginning of Year Contribution	Account Balance at 8%	Tax Savings at 28%	Tax Savings Reinvested at 8%	Combined Accounts
45	2,000	2,160	560	0	2,160
46	2,000	4,493	560	605	5,098
47	2,000	7,012	560	1,258	8,270
48	2,000	9,733	560	1,963	11,697
49	2,000	12,672	560	2,725	15,397
50	2,000	15,846	560	3,548	19,394
51	2,000	19,273	560	4,437	23,710
52	2,000	22,975	560	5,397	28,372
53	2,000	26,973	560	6,433	33,406
54	2,000	31,291	560	7,552	38,843
55	2,000	35,954	560	8,761	44,716
56	2,000	40,991	560	10,067	51,058
57	2,000	46,430	560	11,477	57,907
58	2,000	52,304	560	13,000	65,305
59	2,000	58,649	230	14,645	73,294
60	2,000	65,500	560	16,422	81,922
61	2,000	72,900	560	18,340	91,241
62	2,000	80,893	560	20,412	101,305
63	2,000	89,524	560	22,650	112,174
64	2,000	98,846	560	25,067	123,913
	40,000		11,200		

Contributions Roth IRA

	Beginning of Year Contribution	Account Balance at 8%
1	2,000	2,160
2	2,000	4,493
3	2,000	7,012
4	2,000	9,733
5	2,000	12,672
6	2,000	15,846
7	2,000	19,273
8	2,000	22,975
9	2,000	26,973
10	2,000	31,291
11	2,000	35,954
12	2,000	40,991
13	2,000	46,430
14	2,000	52,304
15	2,000	58,649
16	2,000	65,500
17	2,000	72,900
18	2,000	80,893
19	2,000	89,524
20	2,000	98,846
	40,000	

TABLE 6-5

(concluded)

Withdrawals Deductible IRA

Age	YR	Beginning of Year Withdrawal	After-Tax Cash Rec'd @ 28% Tax Bracket*	YR	Beginning of Year Acct. Bal.	Beginning of Year Withdrawal	End of Year at 8%
65	21	13,404	9,860	21	123,913	13,404	119,349
66	22	13,404	9,860	22	119,349	13,404	114,421
67	23	13,404	9,860	23	114,421	13,404	109,098
68	24	13,404	9,860	24	109,098	13,404	103,350
69	25	13,404	9,860	25	103,350	13,404	97,141
70	26	13,404	9,860	26	97,141	13,404	90,436
71	27	13,404	9,860	27	90,436	13,404	83,195
72	28	13,404	9,860	28	83,195	13,404	75,374
73	29	13,404	9,860	29	75,374	13,404	66,928
74	30	13,404	9,860	30	66,928	13,404	57,806
75	31	13,404	9,860	31	57,806	13,404	47,954
76	32	43,404	9,860	32	47,954	13,404	37,314
77	33	13,404	9,860	33	37,315	13,404	25,823
78	34	13,404	9,860	34	25,823	13,404	13,412
79	35	13,404	9,860	35	13,412	13,404	9
		201,060	147,900				

Withdrawals Roth IRA

YR	Beginning of Year Acct. Bal.	Beginning of Year Withdrawal	End of Year at 8%
21	98,846	10,692	95,206
22	95,206	10,692	91,275
23	91,275	10,692	87,030
24	87,030	10,692	82,445
25	82,445	10,692	77,493
26	77,493	10,692	72,145
27	72,145	10,692	66,370
28	66,370	10,692	60,132
29	60,132	10,692	53,395
30	53,395	10,692	46,119
31	46,119	10,692	38,261
32	38,261	10,692	29,775
33	29,775	10,692	20,610
34	20,610	10,692	10,711
35	10,711	10,692	20
		160,380	

*Note: 28% income tax is levied on a total of $201,060 of withdrawals, less the $11,200 of reinvested tax savings (which is tax free). Therefore, there will be (($201,060 − $11,200) x .28) = $53,161 of total income tax paid. On average, there will be ($53,161 / 15 years) = $3,544 of annual income tax due. Therefore, there will be a total of ($13,404 − $3,544) $9,860 of after-tax cash proceeds received per year, or ($9,860 x 15) $147,900 of total after-tax proceeds received.

5. PHASED-IN INCREASE IN THE FEDERAL UNIFIED CREDIT

In 1997, the estate of every U.S. citizen and U.S. resident is entitled to a $192,800 unified credit against all federal gift and estate taxes. Currently, the exemption equivalent dollar value of the unified credit is $600,000. Therefore, during life, a person can make gifts of up to $600,000 without gift tax or may bequeath up to $600,000 of property to heirs without paying a federal estate tax. The new tax law increases the exempt amount gradually from $600,000 to $1,000,000 by the year 2006.

Trap Over time, your estate may grow faster than the amount protected by the unified credit. An estate worth $600,000 will grow to $1,000,000 in nine years at an annual growth rate of 5.84 percent. The $600,000 unified credit will grow to $1,000,000 over the next nine years. This represents only a 5.84 percent annual increase in estate protection. The marginal estate tax rate on the next dollar over $1,000,000 is 41 percent.

As shown in Table 6–6, under the new tax law, the current unified credit of $192,800 will be increased to $345,800 over the next nine years. As a result, the amount of property sheltered from estate or gift tax will increase from $600,000 to $1,000,000 over that same period. The overall increase in the unified credit is $153,000 ($345,800 less $192,800), and the overall increase

TABLE 6–6

Unified Credit Under the New Tax Law

Year of Death	Unified Credit	Exemption Equivalent	Increase in Exemption Equivalent
1997	$192,800	$ 600,000	$ 0
1998	202,050	625,000	25,000
1999	211,300	650,000	25,000
2000	220,550	675,000	25,000
2002	229,800	700,000	25,000
2004	287,300	850,000	150,000
2005	326,300	950,000	100,000
2006	345,800	1,000,000	50,000

in the amount of property protected against tax increases is $400,000 ($1,000,000 less $600,000).

Trap   Existing wills and living trusts must be reviewed. If you have a will that creates a bypass or credit shelter trust, the increased unified credit will automatically change the distribution of your property to heirs at your death. Consult with advisors to determine if this is what you really want.

If you have a will that creates a bypass or credit shelter trust at your death, the new unified credit will increase the funding of that trust. By the year 2006, the trust could be funded with $1,000,000 at your death. For medium-sized estates, this may leave a surviving spouse with a smaller outright inheritance than he or she desires.

Take the example of a decedent whose estate in the year 1997 is valued at $1,200,000. Under the terms of his will, a bypass or credit shelter trust will be funded with the maximum amount available under the unified credit. Under 1997 law, this trust would be funded with $600,000 of assets and the remaining $600,000 would be distributed outright to the surviving spouse, free of estate tax, under the unlimited marital deduction. Under the new law, the identical estate might be distributed quite differently. In the year 2006, a bypass or credit shelter trust could be funded with up to $1,000,000 of assets, leaving only $200,000 for the surviving spouse.

> Over time, your estate may grow faster than the amount protected by the unified credit.

The $200,000 may be sufficient only to pass on a qualified retirement plan or IRA and some personal property. That's not very much. In other words, the law change may leave the surviving spouse with a pension and some personal property as an inheritance, with everything else held in trust. This may not be satisfactory. A careful estate review may uncover this kind of problem. Life insurance is often used to increase the amount of cash received by a surviving spouse. If the surviving spouse spends this death benefit (as opposed to saving it), it will not increase the spouse's estate.

The increased protection of the unified credit is not a reason to avoid estate planning. Rather, it should be a catalyst for new planning or for reviewing previous planning. Consider the following strategy.

Strategy Use the current and future increases in the unified credit to make gifts to children of shares in your business or of cash to fund life insurance programs that help pay your estate taxes. Making gifts during your life can reduce the future growth of your estate and potentially lower your estate taxes.

Table 6–7 shows the estimated tax savings that can be realized over time by making gifts during life equal to the unified credit exemption equivalent.

If death occurs in the year 2006, Table 6–7 shows that gifts protected from tax under the unified credit over the next nine years, if invested at an 8 percent annual after-tax growth rate, remove $830,779 of value from your estate and save $456,927 of estate taxes—assuming your estate were in a 55 percent top tax bracket.

TABLE 6–7

Estate Taxes Saved By Making Gifts of the Unified Credit

Year	Gift of Exemption Equivalent	Growth Removed from Estate if Gift Grows @ 8% After Tax	Estate Taxes Saved on Growth @ 55% Bracket
1997	$ 600,000	48,000	26,400
1998	25,000	101,840	56,012
1999	25,000	161,987	89,092
2000	25,000	228,946	125,920
2001	0	301,262	165,694
2002	25,000	381,362	209,749
2003	0	467,871	257,329
2004	150,000	573,301	315,315
2005	100,000	695,165	382,340
2006	50,000	830,779	456,927
	1,000,000	830,779	456,927

Generation-Skipping Estate Planning

Under current law, every U.S. citizen or U.S. resident is entitled to a $1,000,000 generation-skipping transfer tax (GSTT) exemption. This exemption permits every person to give up to $1,000,000 to grandchildren generation skipping tax free (although gift and estate tax may apply). After 1998, this exemption, along with the $10,000 gift tax annual exclusion, will be indexed for inflation. Once the unified credit exempt amount reaches $1,000,000, it will then be possible to give $1,000,000 to grandchildren (outright or in trust) *without paying income tax, gift tax, or generation-skipping transfer tax.* Furthermore, with proper planning, if some of these gifts are leveraged as premiums for life insurance, the end result could be that literally millions of dollars are received by grandchildren at the death of a parent or grandparent—tax free.

6. ESTATE EXCLUSION FOR FAMILY-OWNED BUSINESSES AND FARMS

Under prior law, owners of family businesses did not receive any special exemption from the federal estate tax. As a result, business owners who wanted to transfer their businesses to children or other family members wound up saddling their families with an estate tax liability. Often, this made it very difficult for the family to keep the business. To help pass on family-owned businesses to the next generation, business groups lobbied vehemently for the repeal of the estate tax. In response to this, and in addition to the increase in the unified credit, TRA '97 attempts to provide special estate tax relief to qualified family-owned businesses. Unfortunately, it may not have succeeded.

Reduced Federal Estate Tax for Qualified Family-Owned Businesses

Owners of family businesses and farms can now exclude from their estates up to $675,000 in value of qualified family-owned business interests owned at death. This exclusion, when combined with the unified credit, can shelter up to $1,300,000 of value from the estate of the owner of the family business. However, the exclusion reduces as the unified credit increases. Thus, the actual exclusion is as follows:

Year	Exclusion
1998	$675,000
1999	650,000
2000	625,000
2001	625,000
2002	600,000
2003	600,000
2004	450,000
2005	350,000
2006	300,000

It is ironic that the new law was drafted in such a way as to cause a wealthy business owner who dies in eight years to actually pay higher estate taxes in 2006 than he would on the same assets had he died in 1998. For example, suppose a business owner has a $4,000,000 taxable estate both in 1998 and in the year 2006 and qualifies for the new estate exclusion. The federal estate tax would be calculated as shown in Table 6–8. This unusual result occurs because for wealthy individuals the decrease in the business exclusion (from $675,000 to $300,000) has a larger impact on the estate tax than does the increase in the unified credit equivalent (from $600,000 to $1,000,000).

Trying to Use the New Family Business Estate Exclusion

Many requirements must be met for a family-owned business to qualify for the new estate exclusion. The most important of these are the following:

1. A family-owned business is defined as one that has a principal place of business in the United States. The business must be owned at least 50 percent by one family, or 70 percent by two families or 90 percent by three families, but in any event the decedent's family must own at least 30 percent for it to qualify.
2. At the time of death, the decedent must have been a U.S. citizen or U.S. resident.

TABLE 6–8

Tax Impact of Increasing Unified Credit and Decreasing Estate Exclusion

	Date of Death 1998	Date of Death 2006
Tentative Taxable Estate	$4,000,000	$4,000,000
Business Exclusion	675,000	300,000
Taxable Estate	3,325,000	3,700,000
Tentative Tax	1,469,550	1,675,800
Unified Credit	202,050	345,800
Estate Tax Due*	1,267,500	1,330,000

*Assumes no other deductions or credits.

3. The value of the decedent's interest in the business must have exceeded 50 percent of his or her adjusted gross estate.

4. The decedent, or another member of the family, must have owned and materially participated in the business for at least five of eight years preceding the decedent's death. A family member is broadly defined as the decedent's spouse, ancestors, lineal descendants, lineal descendants of the decedent's spouse, the spouses of the decedent's lineal descendants, and the lineal descendants of a partner of the decedent.

Many Business Interests Won't Qualify

Many businesses will not qualify for the family business exclusion. A business may not qualify as a family-owned business because it is owned by too many families, or the value of the business interest at death does not exceed 50 percent of the decedent's adjusted gross estate, or because of the inability of the decedent's family to meet the material participation requirements.

Trap   It is possible for a business to qualify for the new estate exclusion at the time the family creates its estate plan and then, for one or more reasons, not qualify for it at the owner's death.

Certain businesses, such as professional corporations, will rarely qualify because a "qualified heir" must be appropriately licensed as a professional. State laws prohibit a lay person (non-professional) from owning a medical or legal practice even if that person is a family member. As an alternative, the new law defines "qualified heir" to include an employee actively employed by the business for at least 10 years prior to the date of the decedent's death, or a family member. This requires having long-term employees who are willing and able to buy or inherit and run the business at the owner's death.

Even if a parent leaves a professional practice to a licensed child, the value of the practice might not exceed 50 percent of the decedent's adjusted gross estate and not qualify for the exclusion. Professional practices are generally valued differently from traditional businesses. Often, their greatest value might be good will and accounts receivable that may not have a high value at death. The deceased professional most likely will have accumulated substantial non-business assets, and the value of the professional practice might not exceed 50 percent of the adjusted gross estate. Another possibility is that the largest asset of many business owners today may be their qualified plan or IRA. The value of these plans may equal or exceed the value of a closely held business and prevent the estate from using the business exclusion.

Estate Tax Recapture

Even if the estate of a deceased owner of a family business qualifies for the exclusion, there is a series of events that can occur within 10 years *after death* that will disqualify the use of the exclusion and trigger a recapture of the estate tax.

These recapture events are as follows:

1. A qualified heir ceases to materially participate in the business.
2. The qualified heir sells, liquidates or otherwise disposes of the business.
3. The principal place of business is moved out of the United States.
4. The qualified heir loses his or her U.S. citizenship.

Amount of Recapture

The amount of estate tax that is recaptured depends on when the disqualifying event occurs. If the event occurs:

- within 6 years of death, the recapture is 100 percent of the tax saved.
- in the seventh year following death, it is 80 percent.
- in the eighth year following death, it is 60 percent.
- in the ninth year following death, it is 40 percent.
- in the tenth year following death, it is 20 percent.

Once the eleventh year is reached, qualified heirs are free to dispose of, sell, or otherwise relocate the business without paying any recapture tax.

Strategy Due to the complexities involved and the numerous rules that must be followed, it will be difficult for families to successfully use the new estate exclusion for family-owned businesses. Consequently, when you plan for the funding of estate taxes, it may be advisable to assume that the new estate exclusion will not be available to your estate. If your estate qualifies, at worst your family will have additional cash for business working capital or to fund additional survivor income.

The new law may give many business owners and their families a false sense of security with respect to paying estate taxes on family-owned businesses. At the time of death, there are substantial requirements to be satisfied in order to prevent the recapture of the estate taxes saved after death. One major concern is that the qualified heirs to the business may have a difficult time maintaining the business even if little or no tax is due. Often, children who buy or inherit a family business do not have the skill, training and business acumen that the founding parent(s) may have had. In other words, the *survival of the business can be jeopardized by poor management.* If the new exclusion is elected, the liquidation of a failed business could cost the family money in the form of recapture taxes.

One way to help a business survive is for new owner(s) to have the financial resources to pay the recapture tax in the event one or more financial or personal contingencies occur.

Otherwise, they may become liable to pay a tax at the precise time when the business is not profitable and cash is tight or non-existent. In addition, a risk of business failure may occur if the owner(s) become disable and are no longer able to materially participate in the company.

One approach that all family-owned businesses should consider is having enough liquidity to pay both current estate taxes (which may be due at the decedent's death) and future potential recapture taxes. Life insurance issued on the business owner's life may be an efficient way for surviving family members to create enough cash to pay current estate taxes and help keep the business going so that the recapture tax is not triggered. The insurance can be purchased to fund a buy-and-sell arrangement at death, or it can be owned by the family as key-person insurance.

7. REPEAL OF PENSION EXCISE TAXES DURING LIFE AND AT DEATH

Under prior law, distributions from qualified retirement plans and IRAs that exceeded a specific threshold amount were subject to an excess accumulations tax of 15 percent. This tax, levied in addition to any estate tax and income tax due, subjected the beneficiary of a qualified plan or IRA to three separate federal taxes! TRA '97 repeals the excess accumulations tax as well as the 15 percent excess retirement distributions tax and reduces the overall tax liability of individuals who have interests in qualified plans.

That's the good news.

The bad news is that as a result of the new law, people will continue to accumulate large tax-deferred sums in their qualified retirement plans that will be taxed heavily at their death. (Note: By the term "large" we mean more money than you will need for your retirement.)

Strategy Individuals who accumulate large amounts in qualified plans and IRAs should buy life insurance to help pay some or all of these taxes. This includes buying insurance in profit-sharing and other qualified plans with pre-tax dollars.

The elimination of excise taxes during life and at death may not provide extensive tax relief and does not address the major tax burden that can occur when someone dies owning large tax-qualified accounts. In reality, the elimination of the 15 percent excess accumulations tax on an estate in a 55 percent bracket is only a reduction in tax of about 7 percent. Why? Under prior law, the triggering of the excise tax created a deduction against the gross estate. For example, suppose a person died in 1996 and the estate had to pay a hypothetical $100,000 excess accumulations tax. That $100,000 would be a deduction against the gross estate for federal estate tax purposes. If the estate were in a 55 percent top tax bracket, the $100,000 payment would save $55,000 in estate taxes. Thus, the additional tax imposed would be only $45,000. If the $100,000 excise tax represented a 15 percent tax, then

> By the term "large" we mean more money than you will need for your retirement.

the actual $45,000 cost would represent a 6.8 percent tax. Despite this fact, the excise tax was still seen as the final tax on top of two additional taxes (the 55 percent estate tax and the 39.6 percent income tax) that made many qualified plan accounts almost worthless to heirs. Under the new law, the major tax burden still remains: Distributions from qualified plans can still be subject to:

- federal estate taxes
- federal income taxes
- state income and death taxes

These taxes can easily exceed half of the plan distribution. As a result, *more money could go to federal and state tax collectors than to your beneficiary.* If your beneficiary is a surviving spouse, however, he or she can defer all taxes by rolling over the money to an IRA or other eligible qualified plan. The major tax disaster occurs when the beneficiary is not the surviving spouse. A non-spouse beneficiary is not allowed to roll over money or use the unlimited marital deduction.

In many cases, a life insurance policy can be purchased inside the plan with pre-tax dollars. But to avoid estate tax on the life insurance, the plan participant may want to eventually retrieve the policy out of the plan. This can be accomplished by assigning it to a trust or a child.

8. NEW 10 PERCENT PASS-FAIL TEST FOR CHARITABLE REMAINDER TRUSTS

Strategy If you are under age 50, be cautious about using charitable remainder trusts (see Chapter 5) to accumulate money for retirement. CRTs designed to provide a life income to younger couples may fail the new 10 percent test.

The new tax law includes a provision that has a significant impact on the use of charitable remainder trusts (CRTs) that are created to maximize retirement income. Under the new law, in order to be a valid charitable remainder trust, a CRT must pass a new test.

TABLE 6–9

Life Income CRTs that Pass or Fail the 10 Percent Test

Unitrust Interest	5%		6%		7%		8%		9%		10%	
Number of Lives	1	2	1	2	1	2	1	2	1	2	1	2
Age 20	F	F	F	F	F	F	F	F	F	F	F	F
25	P	F	F	F	F	F	F	F	F	F	F	F
30	P	F	F	F	F	F	F	F	F	F	F	F
35	P	P	P	F	F	F	F	F	F	F	F	F
40	P	P	P	F	F	F	F	F	F	F	F	F
45	P	P	P	P	P	F	P	F	P	F	F	F
50	P	P	P	P	P	P	P	F	P	F	P	F
55	P	P	P	P	P	P	P	P	P	P	P	P
60	P	P	P	P	P	P	P	P	P	P	P	P
65	P	P	P	P	P	P	P	P	P	P	P	P

P = Pass   F = Fail

Note: This chart is presented for illustrative purposes only and should not be relied on in place of an exact calculation, which must be made by a client's personal tax advisor.

In simple terms, the test is whether or not the *present value of the remainder interest in the property going to charity is at least 10 percent of its current fair market value.* This 10 percent "pass-fail" test began to apply to all contributions to new and existing CRTs after July 28, 1997.

The new rules may prevent young people from contributing property to new and existing CRTs if the trusts are designed to provide a life income for one or more lives. The rules are summarized in Table 6–9. An "F" means that a CRT failed the test and is not valid. A "P" means that the CRT passed the test and is valid. As you notice, the higher the retirement income rate and the younger the contributor is, the more likely it is that the trust will fail.

Strategy   Continue using CRTs for estate planning when highly appreciated long-term capital gain assets must be sold and converted to assets that produce higher income.

9. INTEREST DEDUCTIONS MAINTAINED FOR BUSINESS LOANS TAKEN BY CORPORATIONS THAT OWN CASH VALUE LIFE INSURANCE

For policies issued after June 8, 1997, no income tax deduction is allowed for interest paid or accrued on any business debt allocable to unborrowed and untaxed cash surrender values on policies owned by the business. One of the exceptions to this rule, however, is very broad. Unborrowed cash values on policies covering 20 percent owners, employees, officers or directors of the trade or business are not taken into account.

Strategy   Continue to use corporate split-dollar arrangements (see Chapter 4) to reduce the annual gifts required to fund large second-to-die insurance policies for estate tax planning covering a 20 percent owner and his or her spouse.

As long as the two insureds of a second-to-die policy are a 20 percent owner and his or her spouse, this important coverage will not affect the deductibility of any interest paid by the corporation on its debt. When the first insured dies, if the surviving insured is not a 20 percent owner of the corporation, consider terminating the split-dollar arrangement if the deductibility of corporate loan interest will be negatively affected.

Strategy   Make sure your business maintains sufficient permanent insurance coverage on the lives of its key employees.

10. IMPROVED SECTION 6166 INTEREST RATES

When an estate includes an interest in a closely held business, the executor may elect to pay the estate tax attributed to that business interest in annual installments, as long as value of the business exceeds 35 percent of the decedent's adjusted gross estate. Payments of principal can be deferred for up to five years, at which time the first of a maximum 10 annual payments becomes due. During the five-year deferral period, interest on the unpaid tax balance is due annually. At the beginning of year six, the tax plus interest is due in 10 annual installments. All interest paid is non-deductible.

- Under prior law, if an estate qualified for the deferral of estate taxes under Section 6166, the deferred estate taxes on the first $1,000,000 of estate value (less the applicable federal unified credit) were subject to a special 4 percent interest rate.
- *Under the new law, the 4 percent rate is reduced to 2 percent.*
- Under prior law, deferred estate taxes on estate values in excess of $1,000,000 were subject to interest at the underpayment rate of IRC Section 6601(a).
- *Under the new law, the rate applied to deferred estate taxes on values in excess of $1,000,000 is reduced to 45 percent of the underpayment rate.*

Improved Section 6166 Rates

Estate Value Subject to Tax	Old Law	New Law
First $1,000,000	4%	2%
Over $1,000,000	Underpayment Rate	45% of Underpayment Rate

Under the old law, the deferred estate taxes subject to the special 4 percent interest rate equaled $153,000.

Example Under Old Law

Federal Estate Tax on the first $1,000,000 of estate value	$345,800
Less: Federal Unified Credit	(192,800)
Deferred taxes subject to 4% interest	$153,000

Under the new law, the deferred estate tax subject to the new 2 percent interest rate is based on taxable estate value. This takes into consideration any business interests that qualify for the new estate exclusion for family-owned businesses as well as the increased federal unified credit.

1998 Example Under New Law

Estate Value	$2,300,000
Less: $675,000 Family Business Exclusion	(675,000)
Taxable Estate	$1,625,000
Estate Tax Before Unified Credit	$ 622,000
Less: 1998 Federal Unified Credit on $625,000	(202,050)
Deferred taxes subject to 2% interest	$ 420,000

When expenses are paid by an estate, they are generally estate tax deductible as an administrative expense.

- Under prior law, annual Section 6166 interest payments could be deducted as an administrative expense.
- *Under the new law, effective for decedents dying after December 8, 1997, Section 6166 interest payments are non-deductible.*

Strategy   Despite the reduced interest rates provided under the new law, Section 6166 is an expensive and potentially dangerous method of paying estate taxes. Here's why:

- For as long as there remain unpaid taxes, the IRS imposes a tax lien on the closely held business.
- If any part of principal or interest is not paid when due, the whole of the unpaid portion of the tax payable in installments must be paid in full.

- If any portion of the business is distributed, sold, exchanged, or otherwise disposed of, or money and other property attributed to the business interest is withdrawn from the business, the unpaid portion of the tax payable in installments must be paid in full.
- Section 6166 interest payments are non-deductible.
- If business income will be used to pay the annual Section 6166 installments, personal income taxes must be paid on this income before it can be used to pay the installments.

11. MISCELLANEOUS STRATEGIES FOR INDIVIDUALS

- *Strategy:* Deduct a part of the cost of your home as a principal place of business. For tax years beginning after 1998, a home office will more easily qualify as a principal place of business if it is used exclusively and regularly by the taxpayer to conduct administrative or management activities of a trade or business and if there is no other fixed location where the taxpayer conducts substantial administrative or management activities of the business.
- *Strategy:* Deduct more of your health care costs. With some restrictions, self-employed individuals can now deduct 40 percent of the premiums they pay for personal and family health insurance. This deduction is scheduled to increase in stages until it reaches 100 percent by the year 2007.
- *Strategy:* For small corporations, completely avoid corporate alternative minimum tax (AMT) on the cash surrender value and death benefits of corporate-owned life insurance. The new law eliminates corporate AMT for small corporations (whose gross receipts do not exceed an average of $5,000,000 per year for the three years preceding 1996. Thereafter, a corporation will continue to be exempt from AMT as long as its average gross receipts for the three-year period preceding the taxable year in question have not exceed $7,500,000).

- *Strategy:* Get a write-off when you give away your company's old computers. For the tax years 1998 and 1999, the rules that permit a charitable deduction for a greater portion of the fair market value of certain corporate property given to charity have been expanded to include gifts of computer equipment to be used in the United States for educational purposes in grades K through 12.

Protecting Your Assets

Avoid the Worst Case . . .
By Planning for It

Key Concepts Revealed in This Chapter

Insurance and Annuity Exemptions
How to Protect against the Threat of Disability
Buy/Sell Agreements Help Protect Your Most
  Valuable Asset: Your Business
Partnership Arrangements

Let's face it: As you set out to build your company—and, in turn, your personal wealth—through the integration of business and personal assets, a million things can go wrong, including

- Fires.
- Bad debts.
- Death.
- Disability.
- Recession.
- Bankruptcy.

Whether these are minor setbacks or major disasters can depend on the level of planning (or lack of it) that goes into protecting your assets.

Take the unpleasant prospect of bankruptcy. Why should an entrepreneur growing a successful business fret about this worst-case scenario? Because it is part of the process of sound financial planning. In today's competitive environment, personal and corporate bankruptcy is an ever-present threat because it can occur in ways never imagined. What's more, big jury awards can result in having your pockets picked by plaintiffs and creditors. With this in mind, you would be wise to explore strategies designed to insulate assets from attack.

Although incorporation is widely viewed as *the* means of sheltering personal assets from business creditors, shareholders of closely held corporations can remain vulnerable to the financial impact of certain lawsuits. How to guard against this? As we've already discovered, one strategy is to give assets to your children. Under the theory "If you don't own it, they can't take it from you," your creditors cannot attach assets that are gifted to others prior to a claim as long as the transfer is not intended to defraud creditors. In making such gifts, irrevocable trusts or family limited partnerships can offer some flexibility and protection. For example, transferring assets to a trust may provide asset protection for you and a lifetime income for your spouse, with the assets distributed to your children upon your spouse's death. This strategy may also minimize or avoid estate taxes, but only works if your spouse is not liable to the creditor.

Qualified pension plans, annuities, and life insurance contracts can also insulate assets from claims of general creditors.

For example, in June 1992, the U.S. Supreme Court ruled that assets held on behalf of a participant in a qualified pension or profit-sharing plan are exempt from claims of the participant's creditors in a bankruptcy proceeding (*Patterson* v. *Shumate,* 112 S. Ct. 2242, [1992]). Note: This ruling may not protect sole or controlling shareholders.

Be aware, however, that the Supreme Court pension ruling did not apply to individual retirement accounts. So, if you have a choice of rolling over qualified pension plan assets into either an IRA or another qualified plan, the qualified plan may offer more protection. State laws (which govern IRAs) present a patchwork of additional rules and regulations you will want to check. These rules vary widely from state to state.

> **Personal and corporate bankruptcy is an ever-present threat because it can occur in ways never imagined.**

The Supreme Court's ruling also does not apply to claims of a spouse, former spouse, or child who may be owed money from a plan participant for alimony, child support, or other property settlement made pursuant to a divorce or other court-supervised dissolution of the marriage.

INSURANCE AND ANNUITY EXEMPTIONS

In many states, the cash values and death benefits of life insurance and annuities are either partially or totally exempt from the claims of creditors. This exemption may depend upon ownership and beneficiary designations. Cash value life insurance may allow you, as the owner, to retain control over your cash value while insulating that cash from your creditors. But even in states that generally exempt insurance from the claims of creditors, individuals facing professional liability claims may be at risk. Likewise, life insurance is not exempt if premiums were paid in fraud of creditors.

Here, you may want to explore a creative strategy to protect business assets: Borrow on your corporation's stock or personal accounts receivable, and use the proceeds to fund personal life insurance and annuities. The lender may have a lien on the stock or retain the right to the receivables, but the policies' cash values are generally exempt from the claims of creditors.

Let's look at a hypothetical example. Suppose a 40-year-old married man who owns a growing company could borrow on his $100,000 of accounts receivable. In the first year he could use all or part of the borrowed money to purchase a high cash value policy. Under one insurance strategy, a business owner could purchase a $975,000 second to die policy with a policy premium of $7,147 payable annually. An additional rider could be purchased which would enable the policy-owner to pay $69,854 into the policy, so that the total outlay in the first year is about $77,000 (your insurance agent can provide you with an illustration of policy values which you should review before purchasing). This insurance program could provide the policy-owner with guaranteed cash value of about $71,000 at the end of the first year. Depending on state law the entire cash value could be exempt from future creditors' claims. Future cash value increases could help offset the cost of borrowing on the receivables.

A word of caution: States forbid transferring cash or other property with the intent to defraud creditors (which is certainly not our goal here). Also be aware that life insurance and annuities owned by corporations and partnerships are not protected from business creditors. It may be prudent to provide for ownership by an individual and/or a trust.

Any of these techniques may provide significant asset protection. The best approach is to discuss these options with your legal and insurance advisors, reviewing your course of action from the standpoint of life insurance, retirement funding, and asset protection. Again, the idea is not to defraud creditors but to provide yourself with the maximum wealth protection allowable by law.

HOW TO PROTECT AGAINST THE THREAT OF DISABILITY

As a prudent business owner, you know that a healthy cash flow is critical to the longevity of your business. But have you ever considered how important your key employees are to your cash flow equation? You should. Their daily contributions help you maintain your company's productivity and profitability. If

TABLE 7–1

Probability of at Least One Person in a Group of Executive and Professionals Becoming Totally Disabled for Three Months or Longer Before Age 65

	Number of People in Group			
Age	**2**	**3**	**4**	**5**
25	36.5%	49.4%	59.7%	67.8%
30	35.4	48.0	58.2	66.4
35	34.2	46.7	56.7	64.9
40	32.9	45.1	55.0	63.2
45	31.1	42.8	52.5	60.6
50	28.3	39.2	48.5	56.4
55	23.4	33.0	41.4	48.7
60	15.0	21.6	27.7	33.4

Source: 1985 Society of Actuaries Disability Termination Study

sickness or injury suddenly takes them off the job, imagine the impact it would have on your business.

Worse yet, where would your business be without you? Unthinkable? Perhaps. Unlikely? Unfortunately not. Statistics tell the story as is illustrated in Table 7–1.

Andrew Carnegie, the great industrialist, once said

Take away my factories, my plants; take away my railroads, my ships, my transportation. Take away my money. Strip me of all these, but leave me my people; in two or three years I will have them all again.

With this in mind, consider this: If you or one of your key employees becomes sick or hurt, two main problems may surface—there may be a detrimental impact on your business, and a personal crisis may occur as living expenses continue but income decreases. Ignore these problems now and you may be faced with the following questions later, after a loss has occurred:

- Can your business afford to compensate a disabled employee for work not being performed? For how long?
- How will the loss affect productivity and revenues?
- How will the morale and loyalty of nondisabled key employees be affected?

- Is there a need to hire a replacement? Can your company afford it?
- Who will tell the disabled employee that your company can no longer continue his or her salary?
- If your business continues compensation to a disabled employee without a formal plan, will the IRS consider this an "ad hoc" benefit not deductible as a business expense? Will it be considered a taxable dividend if paid as a disability benefit to you because you are a shareholder?

Now is the time to protect the business you worked so hard to build against the financially devastating impact of a disability that could be suffered by you or one of your key employees. How to accomplish this? Establish a wage continuation plan funded with disability income insurance. With such a plan in place, compensation paid to disabled employees (including yourself as a C corporation business owner/employee) is a deductible business expense as long as the compensation is reasonable.

> Now is the time to protect the business you worked so hard to build.

To establish a plan, draft a resolution adopting the wage continuation plan. Then draft and distribute letters announcing plan benefits to covered employees before the onset of a disability. Next, purchase disability income policies on covered employees.

Advantages of an Insured Plan

- Premiums are paid when you and your key employees are at work generating revenues.
- You decide who will be covered by the plan and who will not. (The plan can be totally discriminatory.)
- A fixed, budgetable expense is substituted for a fluctuating liability.
- *Disability* is clearly defined in the insurance policy.
- The amount and duration of disability income benefits are guaranteed by the insurer.

- Premium payments are a tax-deductible business expense.
- Risk is shifted to an insurance company.
- Employee loyalty and morale are promoted.

Additional Points

- Formal wage continuation plan premiums paid by an employer are deductible, providing benefits are payable directly to the employee and not the employer. What's more, employees need not include the employer's contributions (i.e., premiums) to a formal wage continuation plan as taxable income (except for employees who are S corporation shareholders, limited liability company owners who own greater than 2 percent of all outstanding shares, sole proprietors, and partners of a partnership).

> Nothing throws a business into turmoil like the death of an owner.

- Benefits received by a disabled employee under a formal wage continuation plan will be taxed as income if the premium has not been treated as taxable income.

As you consider the threat of disability and the need to protect against it, remember the high probability of disaster striking—and remember what Andrew Carnegie said!

BUY/SELL AGREEMENTS HELP PROTECT YOUR MOST VALUABLE ASSET: YOUR BUSINESS

Nothing throws a business into turmoil like the death of an owner. And in many cases, this is more than a management fiasco. The wealth the business represents can be severely jeopardized by the death of an owner. Unfortunately, this is a common scenario. Consider the story in the accompanying box. The episode illustrates another example of how your assets can be jeopardized and what can be done to protect them.

The story of George's One-Day Dry Cleaners is fictional, but the situation is all too common. Fewer than half of all business owners have selected successors, and only one in three has

GEORGE'S ONE-DAY DRY CLEANERS

Whenever anyone thought of George's One-Day Dry Cleaners, they thought of the founder and president, George Smith. Starting the business from scratch, George built a clientele that supported the company's growth, enabling him to expand from a single shop to a thriving chain. He knew the business, and his suppliers respected him. When George planned his expansion, creditors were confident that he was a solid risk. He was a natural manager, skilled at motivating employees. The company's potential appeared to be unlimited.

Then George died.

A week after the funeral, his wife, June, went to the main shop to take over as manager of the business. June was an intelligent, capable woman, but she knew little about George's One-Day Dry Cleaners. She and her husband rarely discussed company matters, and he left no instructions on how to succeed him. Unintentionally, George had made himself irreplaceable. June, determined to do her best, applied herself to the challenge.

Shortly thereafter, the situation deteriorated. Sally Jones, manager of one of the company's branch stores, quit to work for a competitor. June remembered George is saying that Sally was the reason the shop was a success, but he never said why. Clearly, something was missing: The other workers were uneasy without George and Sally around. In the midst of this crisis, the banker who had financed George's One-Day Dry Cleaners over the years called to request a meeting. She told June she believed the business would not make it without George and that June should consider selling.

June's mind raced. Could she run the family business? Could she sell it? If so, how much was it worth? She thought about the time George discussed the value of the business and had made a personal appraisal of $1,500,000. He had mentioned a buyout offer from Bob Kleen, a successful competitor. Considering her poor negotiating position (without George's skills and with the business deteriorating), June figured she would be lucky to get even $750,000.

But just as everything hit bottom, Kleen called to offer his condolences. He had just returned from a business trip. Then came the surprise: He and George had done more than discuss a buyout—they had structured a so-called *buy/sell agreement*, which provided for this worst-case scenario. In the event of George's death, Kleen would purchase the business for $1,500,000, with

Concluded

the transaction funded with life insurance. And if Kleen died first, George would purchase Kleen's business from his estate at an agreed-upon price. Under current tax law, June could receive this money free of both income taxes and estate taxes.

George had planned to tell June about the buy/sell agreement but had never gotten around to it. He also planned to tell his banker and his employees, including Sally, but that also had fallen through the cracks.

a strategic succession arrangement in place. This poses a serious problem. Uncertainty about the appropriate terms and procedures for business succession can lead to ill feelings and confusion. When an irreplaceable leader is no longer at the helm, expenses mount and revenues sink. That's why buy/sell agreements, which are designed to pass the ownership of a business from one party to another in the event of death or disability, are invaluable.

Our example illustrated a buy/sell between competitors. Competitors are the most likely successors to your business when the company is not passed or sold to family members, key employees, or co-owners.

> **Fewer than half of all business owners have selected successors, and only one in three has a strategic succession plan in place.**

There are generally two ways to establish a buyout agreement. (a) cross purchase buy/sell and (b) entity purchase buy/sell (also known as a stock redemption buy/sell in corporate situations and liquidation if the entity is a partnership):

1. A cross purchase buy/sell is an agreement in which the remaining owner(s) agree(s) to buy the ownership interest of a deceased or disabled owner.

2. An entity purchase or stock redemption buy/sell is an agreement in which the business itself agrees to buy the ownership interest of a deceased or disabled owner (inapplicable to a sole owner).

One key component of a buy/sell agreement is a provision that makes sure the agreement is funded. Proper funding provides surviving business owners or other buyers with enough cash to buy the deceased owner's interest in the business from his or her estate. A Smart Assets strategy is to insure each business owner with enough life insurance that the surviving owners have enough cash to buy the decedent's share of the business from the decedent's estate. Without adequate life insurance, a person who is required, by agreement, to buy part of the business, may be forced to use valuable business or personal assets or borrow to fulfill his or her obligation under the agreement. Alternatively, the buyer may be forced to pay the purchase price over a long installment period due to lack of funds. Each of these options can create dangerous risks that either party may not want to assume, such as

1. *Default risk*—The buyer does not have the cash to buy the business and is unable to raise the cash and cannot fulfill his or her obligation to buy.

2. *Business risk*—The buyer must use important business capital, which may affect future profits.

3. *Credit risk*—The buyer must borrow the money and pay interest, which may affect future cash flow.

4. *Payment risk*—The seller (the estate) must assume that the buyer can make installment payments, and won't die during the process.

5. *Market risk*—The seller may have to assume market risk to sell the business if the buyer is unable to purchase.

The buy/sell agreement can be fundamental to helping preserve the personal wealth of the deceased business owner and the surviving business owners. For the decedent's family, the buy/sell agreement enables them to convert a valuable fixed asset—a business—into cash. This cash can be reinvested for income or growth or used to purchase a new business. For the surviving owners, the buy/sell agreement preserves the business for themselves and their families. After the sale, the surviving owners can focus on their needs without having to account to the decedent's estate or to surviving family members.

The only potential downside of using life insurance as a funding vehicle is the expense of paying premiums. In most situations, you will discover that premiums are affordable and that the life insurance benefit more than justifies its cost, especially if it develops high early cash value.

The two basic corporate buy/sell arrangements are stock redemption and cross purchase. There are important tax and financial differences between them. These differences are important to the buyers of the business.

To illustrate the differences between a stock redemption and cross-purchase arrangement, let's review another hypothetical example. John and Sue are the equal owners of a computer supply corporation. They started the business 10 years ago when each shareholder contributed $50,000 of capital. Today, the business is worth $1,000,000.

John and Sue enter into a buy/sell agreement that is funded with $500,000 of life insurance on each of their lives. They select the stock redemption type of agreement, which obligates the corporation to purchase (redeem) John's or Sue's stock upon the first death. Let's assume John dies first. At John's death, Sue will end up owning 100 percent of the outstanding stock. They buyout is illustrated in Figure 7–1.

As the diagram illustrates, if John dies first, the corporation receives $500,000 of life insurance proceeds, which is then used to redeem John's stock from his estate. John's estate receives cash, and Sue becomes the sole shareholder of the corporation, which is now worth $1,000,000. So far John and Sue have benefited from using these Smart Assets strategies:

- They entered into a buy/sell agreement.
- They used life insurance to fund it.
- John's estate gets the insurance money.
- Sue get the business.

If, sometime in the future, Sue decides to sell the business, she will have to pay a capital gains tax on her profit. In our example, Sue retains her original cost basis in the company, which is $50,000. If she sells the business for $1,000,000, she realizes a profit of $950,000 and must pay a capital gains tax of at least $266,000 (at a 28 percent rate).

FIGURE 7–1

Stock Redemption Illustration

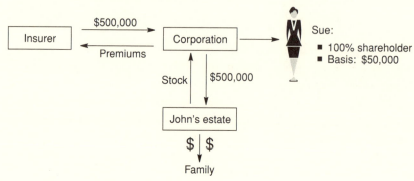

With a different type of buy/sell agreement, it is possible for Sue to avoid more than half of this tax liability when she sells the business. John and Sue could enter into a cross-purchase buy/sell agreement instead of a stock redemption agreement. Under a cross-purchase agreement, Sue will be the owner and beneficiary of a $500,000 life insurance policy on John's life, and John will be the owner and beneficiary of a $500,000 life insurance policy on Sue's life. Upon John's death, Sue receives the $500,000 of insurance proceeds income tax free and uses the money to purchase John's stock from his estate. This arrangement is illustrated in Figure 7–2.

Under the cross-purchase agreement, Sue's cost basis in the business will increase by $500,000. This happens because she personally buys John's stock from his estate for $500,000. This means that her total cost basis in the business will be $550,000 ($500,000 plus her original basis of $50,000). If she sells the business after the buyout, she realizes a capital gain of only $450,000 and pays a capital gains tax of only $126,000 (28 percent bracket). In other words, this Smart Assets strategy (using a cross-purchase arrangement instead of a stock redemption) could save the surviving owner more than $140,000 in taxes upon a subsequent sale of the business.

A cross-purchase agreement can also avoid another potential tax problem when it is funded with life insurance. As a general rule, the death proceeds of a life insurance policy paid to

FIGURE 7–2

Cross-Purchase Buy/Sell Agreement

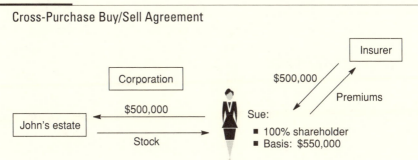

a corporation is not subject to income tax. However, if the business is a C corporation, the death proceeds of the policy may be subject to the alternative minimum tax (AMT). The effect of AMT is that the corporation may have to pay income tax on the death benefits as much as 15 percent. However, the Taxpayer Relief Act of 1997 has eliminated the corporate AMT for many "small" corporations. See page 144 for the details of this change in law. It should be noted that S corporations are not subject to the AMT.

A stock redemption agreement should also be avoided if the corporation owned by members of the same family because the redemption of a family owner's stock could be treated as a taxable dividend under a tax called the "family attribution rules." In a family business, for purposes of a stock redemption, shares of stock owned by family members can be attributed to the decedent. This can prevent the corporation from buying all of the decedent's stock. To avoid family attribution, the corporation must redeem *all* of the shares of stock owned by the decedent, including shares actually or constructively owned by beneficiaries of his estate. This is not feasible if the decedent owns shares of stock constructively. While there are ways to waive family attribution rules, the Smart Asset strategy would be to use a cross-purchase agreement to avoid it completely.

Stock redemption agreements can also trigger a third unforeseen problem. If the company possesses debt, it usually must be repaid before the business can redeem a shareholder's stock. A Smart Asset strategy may be to purchase additional life insurance on the shareholders' lives and use the death

proceeds to repay the debt. This will free up the company's sur-
plus and allow the redemption to proceed. The last thing business owners want would be for existing corporate creditors to
take the insurance proceeds that are earmarked for business
succession planning.

PARTNERSHIP ARRANGEMENTS

If the business is a partnership, entity (or liquidation) purchase
agreements are generally recommended because a portion of
the payouts to the seller or his estate are deductible for the
remaining partners to the extent that accounts receivable and
goodwill represent a portion of the partnership's worth. Payouts
from corporate buy/sells of any type are nondeductible.

A fully funded, properly prepared buy/sell agreement can
solve myriad problems and address a number of critical issues:

- It predetermines the price at which the business owners
  agree to buy and sell their business interests.

- It creates a market for each owner's business interest.

- It can establish the value of each owner's business
  interest for federal estate-tax purposes.

- It can assure creditors and employees of the continuation of the business in the event of an owner's death
  or disability.

- It provides continuous income to a disabled business
  owner without adversely affecting working capital.

- It can provide the money needed to fund the arrangements by using life insurance and disability income
  coverage.

The form of the ideal buy/sell agreement depends on the
size, type, and characteristics of your business. After an accountant or appraiser helps you determine the fair market value of
the business, ask your attorney to draft the agreement. In addition, talk with your life insurance agent about fully and properly funding the agreement with life insurance and disability
income coverage. As the case of George's One-Day Dry Cleaners
illustrates, a carefully structured, predetermined, and regularly
reviewed buy/sell plan is fundamental to wealth protection.

Although buy/sell agreements generally work well, there is a hitch. Premiums paid by either business owners or their companies to fund the agreements are not generally tax deductible. This could prompt some entrepreneurs to forego buy/sell agreements. If you are in this camp, or are inclined to be, you may want to reconsider. The IRS has issued private letter rulings, suggesting that buy/sell agreements may be funded using proceeds from qualified profit-sharing or 401(k) plan accounts—and only those types of accounts. Pension plans and/or IRAs are not eligible for this strategy. This may light the way for the creative funding of buy/sell agreements.

> A fully funded, properly prepared buy/sell agreement can solve myriad problems.

Here's how it works: In a profit-sharing or 401(k) plan, each business owner has an individual or allocated account. The plan trustee uses money in the plan account to purchase life insurance on the other owners' lives and pays the death benefits to all surviving owners. This payment will enable the surviving owners to buy the deceased owners' shares of the business.

The chief benefit of this arrangement is that the premiums are effectively tax deductible. As you know, contributions to a qualified profit-sharing or 401(k) plan, including that portion used to pay insurance premiums, are tax deductible (up to established limits). This effectively means that the government is subsidizing the funding vehicle used to purchase the deceased's equity.

Consider this example: Frank Wilson and Ellen Barnes are co-owners who have built their 100-employee retail company, Wilson-Barnes, into a profitable operation. The owners' corporate benefits include a qualified profit-sharing plan that both Frank and Ellen use to fund retirement. In this context, Wilson-Barnes makes tax-deductible contributions to Frank's and Ellen's accounts. The plan trustee invests the money in a diversified portfolio of mutual funds and personal life insurance payable to the families of the insured.

Frank and Ellen, both essential to running the business, are aware that the survivor would face hardship should either one die. In addition to the problems of managing the business

CAVEATS TO CONSIDER

- To avoid unfavorable tax treatment, only the pure death benefit—not the part equal to the cash value—of the life insurance should be distributed to the survivor. To help avoid a penalty tax, any cash value should be left in the account until retirement.

- The IRS puts limits on life insurance purchases within profit-sharing or 401(k) plans: up to 49.999 percent of cumulative employer contributions allocated to an employee's account can be used to purchase traditional whole life insurance (25 percent for term or universal life). These restrictions, however, are waived on monies that have been in a participant's profit-sharing account for at least two years, and there generally is no limit on premiums (even on less than two-year-old money) if the participant has been in the plan for five years. Frank will only be currently taxed on the annual "term" or P.S. 58[1] value of the death benefit on Ellen and vice versa.

---

[1]Arbitrary term rate for the value of life insurance, made by the IRS for income tax purposes.

alone, under ordinary circumstances the survivor would be forced to (*a*) negotiate the purchase of the deceased owner's share of the business from his or her heirs and (*b*) raise the funds to buy out the former owner's share.

This would be difficult both emotionally and professionally as well as time consuming and disruptive to the business. That's why a buy/sell plan that prearranges the terms of a stock sale in the event of death is a wise approach. In this case, Frank and Ellen would create a cross purchase agreement that sets the price at which the owners would buy and sell their shares of the business, thus providing for a smooth transition and helping ensure continuation of the company. Funding to implement the arrangement would be provided by life insurance.

As part of this process, Frank and Ellen can get double duty from the profit-sharing or 401(k) plan contributions made by the corporation to their accounts if it is handled properly.

After amending their plan, the owners direct the trustee to purchase life insurance on each owner. The policy on Frank's life would be designated by the trustee to be owned by Ellen's account (and vice versa). The plan trustee would serve as nominal owner and beneficiary of the insurance contracts.

Assume Frank dies first. Once the life insurance proceeds are in the plan, the trustee would distribute the death benefits to Ellen, who would use the funds to complete the purchase of Frank's share of the business from Frank's estate. Because premiums for the insurance were paid by the plan, they were purchased on a tax-deductible basis. What's more, the death benefits paid to Ellen are income tax free, thus providing the second of the two tax advantages.

To set up a tax-deductible buy/sell agreement, the business's existing profit-sharing plan documents must allow each participant to direct the trustee to purchase insurance on anyone in whom they have an insurable interest and provide for distribution of policy proceeds (in excess of the cash value) to the participant's account. Plan amendment may be required to accomplish this objective. Some key planning points are described in the above box.

The bottom line is that the tax-deductible buy/sell agreement can help prevent a nightmarish business succession episode for your heirs, your co-owners, and your company.

8

Growing Your Business

Key Concepts Revealed in This Chapter

Financing Your Company
Managing Your Company
Eye on the Bottom Line
Learn from the Legends
Spend Money to Make Money
Summary

Your business is the crown jewel of your assets, the foundation of your wealth. Given its tremendous importance to your financial status, you will want to do everything possible to keep growing the business over the years. This is critical to leveraging the power and potential of your wealth machine.

As you move toward this objective, you will want to focus your attention on two major issues that impact your company's growth and profitability: financing and management. Let's review them one at a time.

FINANCING YOUR COMPANY

In business, success has a price tag of its own. That's because as a company grows, so does its appetite for capital—capital to buy new equipment, hire staff, expand facilities, and purchase inventories. Will you have the money to keep fueling the engines of growth? Only if you know how to succeed with lenders as well as you do with customers. To do so, you will have to recognize that borrowing is an art and a science. The more you know about taking the right approach, the more likely you are to secure business-building cash.

> Many banks base their decisions on the "five P's" of borrowing: personnel, purpose, payment, protection, and perspective.

This isn't as simple as it sounds. In fact, it can appear confusing and illogical. For example, two companies, apparently similar in every regard, approach a bank for a loan. One walks away with a check; the other gets little more than a "Sorry, better luck next time." A mystery? Not really. In all likelihood, the companies weren't as similar as they appeared on the surface, and their differences had a major impact on the bank's decision making.

How were those decisions formed, and what will you face when you apply for business-building capital? Although all banks have their own lending criteria, many base their decisions on the so-called five P's of the prospective borrower's application:

personnel, purpose, payment, protection, and perspective. When applicants rank differently based on these criteria, their chances of securing adequate funding vary substantially. Let's take a closer look at the five P's and see how they figure into the lending decision:

1. *Personnel:* Because they wear so many hats—from chief executive to company cheerleader—small business owners are more critical to their companies' success than their counterparts in the Fortune 500. That's why bankers feel strongly about lending money to experienced and talented entrepreneurs.

   Most important, they must prove their ability to run profitable companies. Academic credentials and personal references have their place, but when it comes to loosening the purse strings, nothing works like a good track record. Second best is to document your performance as a successful corporate manager with real bottom-line accountability. In either case, a reference from an accountant or attorney known to the bankers can add third-party credibility to your qualifications.

2. *Purpose:* How will the money be invested? To bankers this is a critical question. Even the most capable entrepreneur can go off on a tangent, seeking to cash in on a consumer fad just as the sales curve peaks and is about to nosedive. Naturally, bankers want to guard against this.

   Here too, solid documentation can demonstrate that your purpose is sound. A market research study or a consumer poll can convince the lending officer that there is demand for your product or service. Investing a few thousand dollars in this support material may prove pivotal to landing a loan—and may be a deductible expense.

3. *Payment:* Clearly bankers want evidence that you can repay the loan you are applying for. Promising to do so isn't good enough. Bankers have heard it all before. To support your pledge, you'll have to provide financial reports, including profit and loss statements for the

past three years and cash flow projections for the
following two to three years.

Financial reports should be prepared by an accounting firm. The best approach is to ask the banker to recommend the accountant(s) for the job. This way you'll
be working with professionals the banker respects.
This adds further to your credibility.

4. *Protection:* As prudent businesspeople, bankers always
   consider the worst-case scenario. What will happen to
   their money if you can't repay the loan? Here's where
   collateral often comes into play. In general, the greater
   the value of the assets you can offer to secure the loan,
   the more likely the loan will be approved. Acceptable
   forms of collateral include property, securities, inventory and receivables, and life insurance. In fact, life
   insurance may be a required form of collateral. When
   pledging assets, bear in mind that the banker appraises
   them at liquidation value rather than market value.

5. *Perspective:* In the final analysis, a loan decision is
   made on the basis of how the individual criteria tie
   together. Bankers will be looking for a business venture
   that equals or exceeds the sum of its parts.

As you proceed with the borrowing process, never rely on
a single banker. By applying for loans at a number of institutions and retaining relationships with these sources over the
years, you improve the odds of keeping the flow of capital open
at all times.

One reason for this multilender approach is that the decision to support your loan application can be highly personal.
Although your company's financial statements are important,
so too is the lender's perspective. Where one banker sees just
enough doubt in a loan application to turn thumbs down,
another may flash the green light. Extending your net to a
wider range of banks boosts the chances of gaining a favorable
decision. Bear in mind these additional borrowing guidelines:

1. Look to banks or finance companies specializing in
   your field or industry. Institutions familiar with the
   risks and rewards in lending to your type of company

are most likely to produce the needed cash. Ask col-
leagues or trade associations for the names of the most
active lenders.

2. Plan ahead for financing needs, putting the wheels in
motion well before the money is needed. This gives you
ample opportunity to shop the lending market and to
act from a position of strength.

3. Avoid stop/start financing. Assume you need a new
computer system. Like many companies, you may lease
the technology, then secure a working capital loan to
hire staff, and then arrange a line of credit to finance
expansion of the business made possible by the more
sophisticated technology. This stop/start financing
forces you to keep going back to the bank for more
money to maintain your momentum. Should you fail to
get any of the components of your financing, the expansion may fizzle out. That's why it's best to estimate
your total needs up front and to seek financing for that
sum from the start. There's no reason to use all the
money until you need it, but at least the capital will be
available when the crunch hits.

4. When waiting for a bank's decision, never assume that
no news is good news. Unseasoned borrowers take a
banker's silence as an indication that a loan is being
approved, but the opposite is often true. Just when the
borrower thinks that the deal is set, he learns, to his
dismay, that the loan is denied. Protect yourself from
this shock by asking the banker when his decision is
expected and follow up on that date. Wise borrowers
never leave anything to chance.

5. Time lending requests to favorable developments in
your business. Propitious events include the signing of
a major contract, the development of a promising product, or a positive trend in sales and profits. Remember,
anything that builds the banker's confidence loosens
the bank's purse strings.

6. Never equate tight money with no money. Even when
the economy is weak and loans are hard to come by, the
capital markets do not dry up. Persistent borrowers

unwilling to take no for an answer expand their sights beyond the banks to alternative financing sources, including factors, finance companies, venture capitalists, government agencies, and private investors.

7. When comparing loan offers, look beyond the interest rate to the amount of available financing and the terms of the loan. Favor the lender offering the best mix of financing features.

8. Extend the search for debt capital beyond commercial bankers (who tend to be at the conservative end of the lending curve) to so-called asset-based lenders (who are often more agreeable to working with marginal companies). Rather than basing their lending decisions on inflexible debt-to-equity ratios, asset-based lenders focus on the value of your assets, including equipment, real estate, inventory, and receivables.

9. Let your banker know when other lenders are pitching for your business—not to boast, but to underline your appeal as a borrower and, equally important, to strike a deal. If the bank agrees to fulfill your financial needs, you'll agree to turn away competitors. Sometimes the best way to win a banker's enthusiasm is to let him know that others are competing for your business.

10. Send lenders samples of your new products, copies of major contracts, and clips of flattering media articles about your company. These positive reinforcements enhance your appeal as an attractive borrower, tend to keep the lender committed to your account, and increase the likelihood of additional financing in the years ahead.

11. When first applying for a loan, have a respected intermediary accompany you to the lenders' offices. Prominent law and accounting firms can be effective allies. Because they have long-term relationships with financial institutions, their credibility can rub off on you. Nine times out of ten, lenders will have more faith in applications that come through respected sources than those submitted by an unfamiliar borrower.

12. Look for creative financing strategies. One option, espe-
    cially well-suited for strong, growing companies is so-
    called *mezzanine capital.*

Mezzanine capital is a type of borrowing that is junior in
repayment obligation to traditional bank financing but is senior
to high-risk equity capital. Because it is at the midway point of
the financing spectrum, it is ideal for companies that need to
raise relatively high-risk capital but want to avoid the substantial equity dilution generally associated with seed capital or
venture funding. Where sources of mezzanine capital require
an equity stake in the business, which is typical in the majority
of these financings, the amount of equity provided is generally
far less than required for traditional venture capital transactions because companies seeking mezzanine capital are generally well beyond the startup phase and, therefore, carry lower
risks for lenders and investors.

Another feature of mezzanine financing involves so-called
puts and calls. Puts are the investor's right to be paid back in
full, which generally comes into play anytime after the capital
has been extended up to a period of five years. Calls, on the
other hand, refer to the company's ability to buy back the mezzanine financing, which can generally be exercised in five years
as well.

These puts and calls involve more than timing issues. For
the transactions to be fair to both sides, a formula must be
established, in advance, for placing a value on the equity at the
time the put or call is exercised. Typically, these formulas reflect
fair market value based on a multiple of sales or earnings, book
or asset values, or an independent valuation performed by a
third-party professional.

Raising mezzanine financing may be the ideal approach in
any of the following situations: (*a*) You've reached the limits of
traditional bank financing and must find new sources of funds.
(*b*) Public equity financing is unavailable because of the weakness in the market for initial public offerings. (*c*) You believe
your company will experience rapid appreciation over the next
5 to 10 years. Instead of selling equity at what will soon appear
to be undervalued pricing, mezzanine financing is used as

bridge capital that will take you to where you can launch a public offering for premium equity prices. In effect, you are waiting for a point where you can sell your stock at a higher price.

Although mezzanine capital can be an attractive financing source for many growing companies, be aware that it is generally available only to those companies able to demonstrate consistent cash flow and an ability to weather economic cycles. Mezzanine capital is available from investment funds, finance companies, and venture capital firms. Consult with a financial professional for a full review of the financing options available to your business.

MANAGING YOUR COMPANY

As you strive to build your business, you have to look beyond the nuts and bolts of ownership to the broader perspective of *managing*. As an entrepreneur, you are likely a can-do risk taker who defies the odds and creates something out of nothing. Admirable qualities, of course, but you may be so addicted to the adventure, the gamble, that you are impatient with the step-by-step process so critical for building your business over the long term. To succeed at this, you have to think and act like a manager, a chief executive officer (CEO). Guts and vision will still be important, but you have to balance these qualities with the stewardship, planning, and people skills that keep an organization on keel as it grows.

> There is a strength in being small—that even the corporate giants are beginning to acknowledge.

What does managing entail? How do you graduate from entrepreneur to CEO? Start by identifying how you make decisions. If you are like most dyed-in-the-wool entrepreneurs, you are surrounded by subordinates who tend to rubber-stamp your decisions. In this isolation, your mistakes are perpetuated over the years. Let's look at the case of a second- generation restaurateur who refuses to change her family-owned restaurant chain's traditional meat and potatoes menu to reflect an influx of younger consumers interested in lighter fare. Supported by managers who fear arguing with the boss, she sticks to her guns, insisting that fish and salads are a fad. Even a marked drop in sales can't budge her. Defining herself as a bull-headed entrepreneur, she refuses to adopt the market-sensitive flexibility that is critical to strong management.

A lost cause? Not at all. But the entrepreneur (and the legions like her) must end her isolation by inviting one or more outsiders (attorney, accountant, banker, life insurance agent) to serve in an advisory capacity, monitoring her performance and suggesting alternative approaches. This "mini board of directors" forces the owner to justify her actions to independent observers. While this may be more frustrating than dealing with a group of "yes people," it also strengthens the management process.

Let's step back for a moment. Do you ever find yourself apologizing for running a small company? Do you ever say, "We'd like to do this or that, but we're only a small business"? If you are accustomed to thinking and talking this way, you may be selling yourself and your company short. There is a strength in being small—a strength that even the corporate giants are beginning to acknowledge.

You see it all the time in the headlines. In recent years, one major company after another has been streamlining and downsizing, all in an effort to decentralize corporate monoliths into a collection of small businesses. Why this widespread change? Because the corporate giants are recognizing that small business can be more agile, closer to its customers, and capable of adapting to a changing marketplace faster and more effectively than the behemoths. In the process, the giants are seeking to imitate the very strength that is inherent in entrepreneurial ventures.

For small business owners and managers, the lesson is clear: As you seek to grow your business, do everything possible to retain the characteristics that have guided it and contributed to its success to this point. For starters, instead of apologizing for being a small company, take proactive steps to keep your company "small"—not in size but in spirit and organizational structure.

With this "small is beautiful" approach in mind, consider the following guidelines:

- Allow a maximum of three reporting relationships between the company's management and the company's customers. Whether it is in sales, service, or billing, make certain that you are close enough to your customers to hear their complaints (unfiltered through layers of employees) and be able to identify their changing needs and requirements. Remember: the less bureaucracy insulating you from the marketplace, the more clearly these critical messages will come through and the faster you can respond to them.

- Carefully select the business concept by which your company can best make its mark, bearing in mind the oft-ignored principle that "less is more." Rather than taking the traditional approach of loading up on a wide range of products and services—on the assumption that the more you have to sell, the greater your sales volume will be—take the opposite tact, carefully selecting niche markets in which you can excel.

  This highly targeted approach affords you the ability to have substantial depth in the limited range of products and services you choose to offer, enables your employees to gain a high level of expertise in these niche markets, and establishes your company's image as a specialist in a given field or industry. The aura of superiority gained from this enables small companies to effectively compete against the corporate giants who have diversified so aggressively that their image is a blur.

- Reduce company policies, instructions, rules, and operating manuals to the absolute minimum. Staying focused on the customer (as opposed to a preoccupation with an internal agenda that serves the bureaucracy but overlooks a company's most important constituents) enables small companies to outperform their giant competitors in decision making, production standards, and delivery time. With this in mind, take a new look at your company's rules and policies, which have likely multiplied over the years, with an eye toward slashing them by 10 to 25 percent.

- Keep challenging yourself to place severe limits on operating budgets, not only in the shoestring years but also
  as the company grows and prospers. With this "lean and
  mean" mentality in mind, forego the temptation to
  indulge in lavish offices and luxury cars. Instead, live by
  the rule that unless an asset can contribute to revenue
  generation, it is likely dispensable. Holding the line on
  costs enables you to pare your prices to the bone, thus
  outbidding competitors that are held hostage to a
  daunting overhead.

The next time you are tempted to apologize for being small,
remember that this characteristic, when used effectively, can be
your most potent weapon.

EYE ON THE BOTTOM LINE

As you seek to grow your company—without forfeiting its traditional strengths—you'll also want to keep your eye on profitability. With this in mind, here's a key question: Does your
company do what it does—be it making paper cups, selling
security devices, or distributing fat-free foods—because it
makes a profit on all its lines of business? Or is it simply a slave
to inertia, doing what it has always done because no one both-
ers to question profitability? The answer may surprise you.

Here's an example: When a family-owned chain of hair
salons experienced steady growth, management reviewed the
business and added an arsenal of products and services
over the years. First, clothing boutiques were opened in the
stores, followed by a line of company-made shampoos, and then
spa services. But much to management's surprise, this ever-
wider diversification took a toll on profitability; while sales
grew steadily, the bottom line contracted. This led to even more
new services—part of the continuing effort to grow earnings—
without a corresponding increase in profits.

Bad luck? Not really. The fact is, the company's woes could
be traced to a form of management myopia. The family failed
to recognize (because it defied conventional wisdom) that for
the company to prosper it had to shrink rather than grow,

reinvesting itself in the process. Why this turnabout? Because while the company excelled at the retail hair-care business, it knew little about making shampoo and running a spa. By shedding these ancillary products and services, including the plant, equipment, and personnel that went with them, the company could focus its efforts on the profitable core business of retail salons. Clearly, less would be more.

In recent years, pruning a business (often called "downsizing") has been viewed as a recessionary tactic designed to cut costs, or worse yet, as an eleventh hour move to fend off the threat of bankruptcy. But shrewd entrepreneurs, consistently focused on profits, should view downsizing as a positive, offensive move taken to keep the company centered on its most lucrative products and services. With this in mind, consider the following moves to maximize profitability:

- Analyze all lines of business to determine precisely where you are making money, losing money, or breaking even. Your accountants can help with this analysis.

- If you are in the red in an area and a realistic assessment offers little hope for a turnaround, prune the unprofitable products or services. Although it may be difficult to admit defeat or to separate yourself from what was once a pet project, the failure to act will drain the company's profits and set a dangerous precedent. If losers are never axed, the company can easily deteriorate into a collection of bad investments.

- You don't have to simply discard your white elephants. A venture, sideline, or subsidiary that makes no sense in your sphere of operations may have value to other companies. For example, the salon chain's shampoo products may be a dog in a one-product, retail-oriented business but may offer powerful synergy for a beauty products company seeking a shampoo to round out its product portfolio. Before liquidating anything, ask investment bankers specializing in small companies if they can sell the business units that no longer fit your core strategy.

- Expand the downsizing approach beyond products and services to the elements of bureaucracy that creep into

every business and inflate overhead. From a profit perspective, you should not have to run harder and harder
just to stay in place. Typical of this syndrome, depart-
ments and functions tend to add personnel over the
years, often without just cause. Sound business practice
calls for annual staff evaluations to identify and root out
excess capacity in the ranks and, in turn, to streamline
the payroll. Keeping a tight reign on labor costs—both
staff and managerial—helps you to remain competitive
in the marketplace and grow the bottom line, which is
always important.

As you set out to shrink your business in order to refocus
and enrich it, always keep the human factor in perspective.
Faced with a downsizing program that sheds products, services,
and jobs, employees may become
frightened and confused; they may
start to think they should leave the
ship before it sinks. To prevent this,
remember to communicate clearly
and consistently, explaining that the
actions you are taking use offensive
rather than defensive measures and
are designed to create a healthier and
more prosperous environment for
everyone.

But what if your company suddenly seems to lose momentum?
Coping with this downturn and finding a way to navigate through it on
the way to a rebound is another criti-

> Shrewd
> entrepreneurs view
> downsizing as a
> positive, offensive
> move taken to keep
> the company
> centered on its most
> lucrative products
> and services.

cal dimension of effective management. Think of it this way:
Just because your business has experienced steady or meteoric
growth, doesn't mean that joyride won't come to an end. When
it does, a management grown accustomed to good news will
have to adjust itself to the setback, working quickly to get back
on course.

The last thing you want to do is panic because the mark of
a good manager is the ability to stay cool in a crisis. Rather than
losing your head, root out the cause of the problem, and search
for ways to correct it. When the answers aren't obvious (and in

the real world that's most often the case), improvise and experiment, trying any number of tactics to breathe new life into your business.

With a few enlightened moves, you can put sales and profits back on this upward spiral. Try the following:

1. Reformulate your advertising. Whether your ad copy is too familiar, the medium is wrong, or you're simply not spending enough money, a mediocre campaign just doesn't generate business.

   Here's a suggestion: Instead of trying to say everything in the space of a single ad, stress one feature about your business that makes it unique or that gives it an edge over the competition. This can be an exclusive line of goods, a creative payment plan, or simply a home delivery service. You know you have something special. Don't keep it a secret. It's your job to keep the marketplace informed.

2. Do something bold and different. If you're bored with your business, imagine how your customers feel. Too often business owners stick to a tried formula (the one they used to found the company), offering the same products and services in a predictable format year after year. While consistency has its virtues, savvy entrepreneurs spice things up by regularly introducing new merchandise lines and novel promotional techniques.

   Take the restaurant best known for its menu of popular staples including burgers, sandwiches, and chef salads. Perhaps patrons have grown tired of this fare. By adding a small selection of daily specials, drawing from current tastes for low cholesterol diets, the restaurateur can bring excitement to the place without destroying the original concept.

3. Turn old customers into new prospects. Those names already in your files—customers who buy from you now or have done so in the past—are usually the most fertile sources of new business. All it takes is a commitment to expand your relationship with them.

The founding partner of a mid-size accounting firm puts things into perspective:

> When our practice turned suddenly flat, I thought immediately of searching the market for new clients. But then after spending a small fortune on a series of ineffective promotions, I discovered we could do better by calling on existing clients, offering them services they'd never used before.
>
> For example, a tax client who has been with our firm for nine years wasn't aware that we could handle his estate planning or could teach his office staff the "ins" and "outs" of using microcomputers. A half-hour presentation outlining our capabilities in these and other areas brought additional fees of more than $30,000. Multiply that by dozens of clients and you can see the potential.
>
> All the partners in this firm are now aware of the possibilities. They've learned that marketing to established clients is a lot easier and a lot more productive than trying to break the ice with someone who knows little about your practice. Now when business turns sluggish, the search for solutions begins inside the practice, where we can capitalize on strong and productive relationships.

When applying first aid to your business, remember the calm, patient approach is most effective. In many cases, a few simple steps can stimulate sales, setting the stage for a decisive turnaround.

As we have demonstrated, successful management requires intelligence, perseverance, and the ability to think and act decisively. But in addition to these oft-cited characteristics, another key factor—let's call it a "sense of balance"—comes into play. What do we mean by balance? In defining the successful business owner, it is the ability to maneuver deftly in four major skill categories: putting problems and opportunities in perspective, dealing fairly with customers and employees, negotiating the fine line between hands-on control and delegation, and generally keeping the

> Successful management requires intelligence, perseverance, the ability to think and act decisively, and a sense of balance.

business on an even keel. Let's take a closer look at these skills and functions:

1. Caught up in the pressures of business, management can be overwhelmed by the issues that face a company, dashing helter-skelter from budding problem to emerging opportunities. As stated earlier, this can lead to running harder and harder just to stay in place—a mode characterized by lots of action but little progress.

   In many cases, this can be traced to a lack of balance or, specifically, the failure to put matters in perspective by establishing priorities. In this environment, each issue competes for attention with equal urgency, leaving management with little indication of where to turn first. To prevent this, leadership must have a plan that spells out the company's goals and how it will seek to achieve them. This serves as a framework for effective decision making, placing problems and opportunities in the context of the plan.

   Does a specific issue demand immediate attention? It all depends on how it ranks in the broader context of pursuing the company's goals. Within this framework, you'll have a built-in mechanism for achieving balance in the decision-making and action-taking processes.

2. As the president of your company and, most likely, its owner, you are the boss. There can be no question about it. But enlightened bosses don't use that vaunted position to behave like kings. Instead, they recognize that they can be most effective serving as cheerleaders, mentors, and coaches, guiding (rather than bullying) their employees to perform at the highest levels.

   This too requires a sense of balance—specifically, knowing when to use the power and prerogatives of a boss (such as establishing the company's quality control standards) and when to extend a helping hand (supporting an employee through a personal crisis). Knowing what kind of behavior is appropriate under varying circumstances takes more than common sense; it's a sign of leadership that can pay big dividends for your business.

3. If you're an entrepreneur, chances are you believe in the axiom, "If you want something done right, do it yourself." Although there may be some truth to this, it is also a sure way to inhibit your business from realizing its full potential. No one can singlehandedly attend to all key issues demanding executive attention. In many cases, this is evidenced not by the inability to juggle a dozen balls (can-do entrepreneurs are often adept at this) but instead by the failure to address both the operational and visionary sides of the business.

   Here again, balance is critical. Even mediocre managers seek to identify the pressing issues of the day, making certain they are being tackled. But the most effective CEOs take a giant step further, looking beyond today, to ensure that the business is making steady progress toward its long-term objectives.

If this division of duties does not come naturally, you can incorporate it into your calendar, and thus make certain it is accomplished, by setting aside time for the category of managerial responsibilities that often falls through the cracks. Whether your weakness is short-term management or long-term visioning, set aside a specific period of the week for this activity, and stick to it. In time, this balance will become a natural part of your management process. In the process, you can avoid the pitfalls often associated with a myopic approach.

LEARN FROM THE LEGENDS

If managing doesn't come easy to you—or you simply want to raise the bar on your performance—we'll close with a bit of inspiration for success. Start by thinking back on American history, particularly the great strides that propelled the nation forward. As you do so, you will remember the names of legendary entrepreneurs. As much as their fabled counterparts in government, academia, and the sciences, these greats of the business world (including Ford, Disney, Paley, and Watson) have served as role models for generations of men and women.

But they can, and should, play an even bigger role. By studying their companies and the way they built and managed them over the years, today's entrepreneurs can employ proven strategies and techniques. Rather than simply acting and reacting, they can create a framework for business operations—one that defines and governs their approach to the entrepreneurial process.

With this in mind, let's review some of the time-tested principles that worked so well for the legendary entrepreneurs and that can guide your business activities.

Less Is More

This seeming contradiction can be vitally important in shaping a company's marketing strategy. The idea is to direct the firm's products or services to a limited market rather than aiming for the universe of potential buyers. This so-called segmentation marshals the firm's resources to achieve a manageable goal and, in the process, creates a clear image in the marketplace. Had McDonald's founder, Ray Kroc, sought to satisfy gourmands as well as fast-food buffs, it is unlikely that the company would have pleased either group.

> Three time-tested principles to guide your business:
> 1. Less is more.
> 2. Two plus two equals five.
> 3. Spend money to make money.

Let's explore this further. Ever feel like you're rowing against the current or that you're struggling to climb a hill, only to slide back a foot for every step you take? If you're in business and the work you do leaves you standing in place, you know the feeling all too well. Hard as it is to admit, your company is going nowhere fast. The question is, "Why?" What happened to the rapid growth that marked your business in the early years? Where is the potential that once seemed unlimited?

Chances are your woes can be traced to any number of problems, but a "lack of focus" is probably at the top of the list. Put simply, you have allowed yourself to depart from the formula on which you founded your business and to which the market responded enthusiastically. Now is the time to return to your roots, reinvesting in the old formula and using it to regain your company's momentum.

As you go about this process, you want to bear in mind the critical concept of "less is more." Typically, as entrepreneurs seek to revive sluggish businesses, they add to their inventories of products and services, believing that the more they have to offer, the more customers will buy from them. However, just the opposite is true. By adding haphazardly to the company's product and service lines and, in turn, by trying to be all things to all people, you may abandon the niche that gave you a competitive advantage in the first place. As you refocus your business, reclaiming this niche must be a top priority.

With this in mind, take the following steps:

1. Build bridges back to the customer groups that comprised your core market and that put your business on the map.

Take the case of a sporting goods merchant who built his business by appealing to outdoorsmen but then expanded from this niche by marketing a full spectrum of sports equipment, including baseballs, tennis rackets, and basketball sneakers. Although this broad-brush approach generated higher sales at the outset, the boom fizzled when national sporting goods chains moved into the community, christening big stores, launching major advertising campaigns, and offering deep discounts. Suddenly, the local merchant, who had enjoyed substantial margins as a niche player, was forced to compete dollar for dollar on every item in stock. Because he had expanded beyond his niche appeal in catering to outdoorsmen, he forfeited his competitive advantage.

Determined to refocus the business, the merchant stripped away more than two dozen product lines added over the years, returning to the outdoors segment that accounted for the company's initial success. This accomplished three key objectives: (*a*) It reduced the need for extensive inventories in the most price-sensitive product lines. (*b*) It rebuilt the company's relationship with core customers. (*c*) It realigned the business to reflect the community's demographics, which featured a high concentration of affluent consumers active in outdoors sports.

2. Train your employees to be specialists.

If you have moved beyond your core market, chances are employees and managers are assigned to handle customer queries on a wide range of issues. Although they may have the best of intentions, knowledge of extensive product and service lines tends to be superficial. Even the best minds are limited in the range of knowledge they can retain and apply toward the pursuit of quality customer service. By focusing on the "less is more" approach—in this case, training employees in a relatively narrow field or specialty—you create a cadre of experts capable of providing superior customer service.

Consider recent developments in the computer consulting field. While generalists are struggling to find a place in an increasingly segmented market, companies that stake out a special niche, such as state-of-the-art guidance in the creation and management of local area networks, are inheriting a groundswell of customer activity. To duplicate this success story in your business, identify an area of expertise that matches your company's marketing goals, and arrange for staff and managers to get intensive training through seminars, instruction books, technical bulletins, vendor updates, and continuing education courses. The expertise they bring to the table will help build and cement strong customer relationships.

Is it time to refocus your business? If instinct and poor financial performance say that you have strayed from your founding concept, you will want to act now to get back on course.

Two Plus Two Equals Five

In planning business expansion, from opening new branches to taking on additional product lines, action should be taken only if the larger entity will be greater than the sum of its parts.

Let's look at a small retailer contemplating a merger with a local competitor. Should the new business simply be bigger than the individual firms, the deal may not be productive. With successful mergers, two plus two must equal five: The merged entity must provide an additional strength that the parties to the merger did not have independently. For example, a merger between two local retailers, one strong in the downtown market and the other a suburban powerhouse, will give each balanced coverage, making them less vulnerable to competition from the national chains.

SPEND MONEY TO MAKE MONEY

The old adage that money goes to money is as true for corporations as it is for individuals. By investing in state-of-the-art technology, efficient plans, and experienced executives, entrepreneurs can outmaneuver giant corporations and, in the process, compete more successfully for customers.

Keep this in mind: Because big corporations are often slow to change, aggressive upstarts can often get a jump on emerging markets and maintain their share even after the giants invade. In recent years, small companies have scored well with this strategy in the computer hardware and software, electronics, and retailing markets. The idea is to identify markets ripe for newer, faster, or more efficient products and services and to invest in facilities capable of providing this competitive edge. Lenders and investors are often willing to finance these opportunities.

As you seek to learn from the legendary entrepreneurs, note that they remained committed to their vision regardless of prevailing skepticism or business reversals. This can-do attitude proved to be the most powerful weapon in their arsenal. It can be yours too, as you move forward—building and nurturing your wealth machine.

SUMMARY

A chief executive officer of a major U.S. corporation once remarked that he never made a bad decision. He went on to say that some of his decisions, when viewed in hindsight, might have been wrong, but they were not necessarily bad when made because action was taken based on the facts and circumstances at hand. The CEO also remarked that bad decisions usually occur only when people fail to make decisions or fail to take any action.

Through seven chapters, *Smart Assets* has discussed many strategies for creating wealth, preserving it, and passing it on to the next generation. These strategies and techniques will not benefit you unless you take action and start the planning process. It's easy to begin, and here's how you do it.

1. Take the time necessary to establish and prioritize your goals. This may require some discussion with your spouse, children, and business associates. It may be impossible to achieve all of your goals at once. But it is critical to articulate all of them and then select the ones that are the most important to you and your family. Concentrate on them. Make sure they are reasonable and reachable. Avoid setting yourself up for failure.

2. Begin the planning process. This can be complicated or simple, depending on how many obstacles you put in your own way. You may need the help and advice of a team of experts, which may include an attorney, accountant, insurance professional, financial planner, trust officer, or financial officer. Usually, one of these experts will become a team leader and will coordinate the work that has to be done. As part of the planning process, learn to rely on the advice of experts, but make the critical decisions yourself, when appropriate. Keep your experts focused by maintaining your own focus.

3. Begin the implementation process. Select the appropriate strategies and financial products, and implement them.

4. Take a step back and review what you've accomplished. Are you on track toward achieving your goals? As time goes on, your goals may change, laws may change, family and business relationships may change, and financial products may change. As these changes occur, you may have to modify your goals or change the strategies or products you've selected. Therefore, it is critical to review your planning on an annual basis.

As the CEO said, there are no bad decisions, except for failing to make them or failing to act. Take the first step. Begin thinking about tomorrow and what's important to you and your family. Start today!

INDEX